Analytical Study of John's Gospel and the Tabernacle

Tabernacle as John's Book Outline

Rodney F. Price, D.Min.

WESTBOW
PRESS®
A DIVISION OF THOMAS NELSON
& ZONDERVAN

WestBow Press books may be ordered through booksellers or by contacting:

WestBow Press
A Division of Thomas Nelson & Zondervan
1663 Liberty Drive
Bloomington, IN 47403
www.westbowpress.com
844-714-3454

All scripture quotations are taken from the King James Version.

ISBN: 978-1-6642-8367-1 (sc)
ISBN: 978-1-6642-8368-8 (e)

Library of Congress Control Number: 2022920961

Print information available on the last page.

WestBow Press rev. date: 04/25/2023

Rodney F. Price, D. Min.
A Baptist Didache.
New England Baptist Bible Schools, N. H.
Boston Baptist College, Boston, MA.
An Introductory Analytical and Commentary of John's Gospel.
Research Guide with Scholar Quotes and WebSites.

The Tabernacle in the Wilderness.

Jesus is our eternal Mishkan.
God dwells in the inner sanctuary – ναός – naos.
The dwelling place of God – מִשְׁכָּן – mishkān.

Preface

The Source: Many years ago, while fellowshipping with a Jewish missionary Pappi Bodine introduced a concept of this Gospel, which became a burden on our heart to pursue.

His premise is that John used the Tabernacle as the outline of his Gospel.

The Tabernacle demonstrated Jesus' labor and plan, providing the provision of salvation.

The Purpose: The author's primary goal is to provide to the Professor/Teacher with materials to aid his instruction in the classroom and pulpit.

First, to provide limited analytics of many verb forms in this Gospel.

Second, to provide additional quotes from grammatical scholars.

Third, to expose the reader to some of the cultural backgrounds of the Gospel.

The Journey:

> The teaching of this material in limited form began in three churches where we served.
> The professors who helped us to focus on this book's purpose.
> The privilege of teaching at Northeastern Baptist Bible Schools, N.H., and Boston Baptist College, Boston, MA.
> The access to the Libraries at Gordon Theological Library and Baptist Bible Seminary– Summit University, Clarks Summit, PA.
> Professor Dr. King encouraged us to pursue the MA. and Doctoral work.
> The desire to see what God said overrides the urge to add to the text with any material.

The Challenge: We started this project over 30 years ago. The gathering of articles, books, websites and commentaries on the Tabernacle and the Gospel became our constant goal.

The greatest challenge was refreshing our understanding of the Greek grammar rules of the Koine text and the translation process of 4 years. Over the years, we gathered many volumes of Greek Grammars/Commentaries that were added to the library, wondering if we would have access to a Seminary library.

Acknowledgments:

First to my wife Greta who edited all my Pastoral and Seminary labors.
Second, Dr. Kenneth Brown for his overwhelming patience in the Greek classes.
Third, Dr. James King encouraged us to finish the Dr. Min. program at Baptist Bible Seminary – Clarks Summit University, PA.
Fourth, Many thanks to Dr. Abede Alexander and Dr. Bill Smith for their encouragement to complete this project and to provide the funds.

The Usability Reading.

A first-year Greek Grammar class will be helpful but not necessary.
Special attention is given to the verb forms. Not every verb is not explained.
The 1611 grammar not corrected, including the added commentary notes.
Modern English grammar rules are not applied.
The Quoted material is by author's name or sourced in Bibliography.
The Unknown Sources **are** not found, however, included as part of our college lectures.
We stand on the shoulders of the professors of Baptist Bible Seminary-Clarks Summit University, PA.

Resources

Studies and the Use of Public Domain Books.
The Greek texts of the Textus Receptus **and the** Byzantine text.
Greek Grammars using *Robertson's Word Pictures & Vincent's Word Studies.*
The Greek Grammar citations are in 11 pt.
A very elementary identification of the verb tenses.
*Always remember who the speaker is and the point-in-time reference.

1. Aorist Tense – This is a punctiliar point-in-time activity.
2. Imperfect Tense – A past action or state which is incomplete.
3. Imperative Tense – Commands
4. Future Tense – The event beyond the present time of the speaker.

5. Perfect Tense – The completed action with continuing effects at a point in time.
6. Pluperfect – Is an action completed before to some past point of time specified or implied is formed in English by the word "had."
7. Present Tense – This is an ongoing activity in the present time of the speaker.
8. Subjunctive – Expresses situations that are hypothetical or not yet realized.

*Voice concerns the relationship between a verb and its subject.

1. Active Voice – The subject causes the action.
2. Middle Voice – The subject is performing the action for oneself.
3. Passive Voice – The subject is the recipient of the action.

The Granville Sharp General Rule.

1. The article identifies, points out, marks out, particularizes, specifies and draws attention to an object or a person.
2. The absence of the article describes, defines, characterizes, and qualifies.
3. When the article occurs with "God, "God's personhood is in view.
4. When the article is absent with God, the divine essence signifies what God is.

The use of "if"

1. 1st Class Condition – "εἰ" with Indicative mood. The speaker assumes a reality and indicates an assumption of truth for the sake of argument.
2. 2nd Class Condition – "εἰ" with Past Tense, Imperative, and the Aorist Tense. The viewpoint of unreality is contrary to actual conditions. A point-in-time activity. The speaker assumes that this is false in conflict with reality.
3. 3rd Class Condition – When ἐάν is used with the Subjunctive states what results will happen, if the conditions are not met at any time in the future.

John's Gospel with a view of the Tabernacle.

John 1:1– 28.

The Furniture of the Tabernacle.
The Curtain/posts of the Four Gospels.
The Four Posts – Matthew, Mark, Luke, and John.

*The Four Gospels support the tri-colored curtain. Father – Son – Holy Spirit.

John 1:29– 51 The Outer Court – Places of Judgments, Sacrifices and Cleansing.
John 1:29– 51 The Altar of Brass.

   Exodus 20:24 –The Altar is filled with earth.
   Exodus 27:1-8 – The Alter is hollow and filled with earth.

John 2:1– 5: The Laver of Brass.

Three types of people that need washing.

   John 3: – The Religious – Nicodemus
   John 4: – The Semi– religious – Samaritan Women
   John 5: – The Crippled faith – A Jew is lacking the desire to trust God.
   John 6: – The Table of Shewbread – Bread of Life.
   John 7: – 12: The Golden Candlestick – Light of World.
   John 11: The Good Shepherd. *John 12:* The Passover, the 11th of Nisan.
   John 13:-16: Commentary *John 17:* The Altar of Incense – Is in front of the curtain of the
      Holy of Holies.
   John 17: The High Priestly Prayer of Jesus – First of the priestly functions.
      The place where the inauguration of Aaron and his sons,
      The need for precise priest's obedience.
      The warning about using unusable incense. See Lev. 10:1.
   John 18: – 19: The Ark of Covenant – High Priest applies the blood of the Lamb.
   John 20: The Most Holy Place – A Place of God's Presence.
   John 21: The Return to the Holy Place – Fellowshipping with Christ.

Apostle John is the author of this Gospel.

John's audience consisted of Gentile believers with little understanding of the Old Testament. Also, to the recent Jewish believers who are familiar with the Tabernacle.

Strictly speaking, the Gospel of John does not name its author. The internal evidence can lead to the conclusion that it is the Apostle.

   1.   The Internal Evidence may argue for an early date pre-70 AD.

2. The Present Tense, as found in John 5:2, "there is," suggests a time when the Gate is still standing, unlike after the destruction by Titus.
3. *John 1:14 ...and we <u>beheld</u> his glory, the glory as of the only begotten of the Father.* – θεάομαι - A careful and deliberate vision.
4. *John 19:35 And he that saw it bare record, and his record is true: and he knoweth that he saith true, that ye might believe.*
5. *John 21:24, 25 This is the disciple, which testifieth of these things, and wrote these things: and we know that his testimony is true. In addition, there are everyone, I suppose that even the world itself could not contain the books that should be written. Amen.*

The Texts of the Gospel.

The texts consist of the K. J. V. 1611, Textus Receptus, and the Majority text-Byzantine.
https://newchristianbiblestudy.org/bible/greek-byzantine-2000

All author quotes are from public domain sources.

The Terminology.

The Tabernacle – שְׁכָּן – mi+shkan – the "m" = to place. Exodus 25:8.
O.T. Tabernacle – 297 times – Tabernacles – 30 Sanctuary – 137 times – Holy Place or Holy of Holies.
N.T. Temple – ieron – ἱερόν – 71 times – includes all the buildings of the Temple grounds. Temple – Matt. 4:5 – ναός – naos – 45 times – The sacred edifice, Holy of Holies.
Matt. 23:16 Woe unto you, ye blind guides, which say, Whosoever shall swear by the <u>temple</u>"ναοῦ" it is nothing; but whosoever shall swear by the gold of the temple, he is a debtor!

N. T. ναός is the O.T. Mishkan – מִשְׁכָּן mi + shakan.
The Tabernacle tells us of God's dwelling in Israel. God then instructs Moses to build the Tabernacle. See Exodus 25:1.
The Tabernacle is referred to in 297 verses. The word occurs 328 times.
The Tabernacle "merely expresses what itself is in fact. God showed Moses the
Tabernacle and instructed him to make everything exactly according to this pattern. We must assume that in the Tabernacle and its furniture, heavenly, realities were to be expressed in the Tabernacle and its furniture to express in earthly forms." *Edited from Keil & Delitzsch*

"There is always room at the top, and there we may stand, beholding, as in a glass, the glory of the Lord. Notice that God said, Come up unto Me.

He longs to have our love and faith; His delights are with the sons of men; at great cost, He has opened the door of access.

"We need God, but God wants us, and therefore the construction of Tabernacle is next arranged, that He may dwell with men upon the earth."

F. B. Meyer www.studylight.org/commentaries/eng/fbm/exodus-24.htm.l

The 50 chapters mention the Tabernacle.

There are at least 40 chapters,13 in Exodus, 18 in Lev. 13 in Num. 2; in Deut. 4
The construction, the ritual, the priesthood, and the carrying of the Tabernacle, etc.

God's eternal desire is to dwell with us.

God is dwelling with Adam and Eve in the Garden. – Genesis 3:8.
God is dwelling with Noah. – Genesis 6.
God is dwelling with Abraham. – Genesis 11.
God is dwelling in the midst of Israel. – Tabernacle – Exodus 25:8.
God is dwelling in the Temple. – 1 Kings 8:11.
God is dwelling in rebuilt Temple of Zerubbabel. – Ezra 6:15.
  God's Shekinah glory was absent in Herod's Temple.
God is dwelling and revealed in Christ. – John 1:12; Hebrews 1:1.
God is dwelling in Christ, reconciling the world. – 2 Cor. 5:19.
God is dwelling in us. – 1 Cor. 3:16; 2 Cor. 6:16; Col. 1:27.
God is dwelling with our new body. – 2 Co r. 5:1.
God is dwelling with us in eternity. – Rev.1:3.

Exodus 24:16 And the glory of the Lord <u>abode</u> [שָׁכַן – shakan] upon the Mount Sinai and the cloud covered it six days: and the seventh day he called unto Moses out of the midst of the cloud.
Exodus 25:8 And let them make me a sanctuary that I may <u>dwell</u> [שָׁכַן – shakan] among them.
Exodus 25:9 Tabernacle – מִשְׁכָּן – mi+shkan – the "m" = to place.
Exodus 19:45 And I will dwell [shakan] among the children of Israel and will be their God.
Exodus 19:46 And they shall know that I am the LORD their God, that brought them forth out of the land of Egypt, that I may dwell [shakan] among them: I am the LORD their God.

Exodus 40:53 And Moses was not able to enter into the tent of the congregation because the cloud abode thereon, and the glory of the LORD filled the Tabernacle. [mi+shakan] ... and <u>dwelt</u> among us – σκηνοω – skienoo.

Revelation 21:3 The Tabernacle – [σκηνή – skhnh] of God where he will dwell <u>σκηνοω.</u> "behold the Tabernacle of God is with me."

"An allusion to the Tabernacle with the Israelites, and the "Shechinah," or divine Majest being in the midst of them, and as an accomplishment of the promise in Ezek. 37:27, in the fullest sense of it; and designs something distinct from the spiritual presence of Christ in his church, as his Tabernacle and Temple, and in the hearts of his people; and from the heavenly glory, or ultimate state of happiness, in which they will be "with him," and that not as in a Tabernacle, but as in a city, which has foundations: the phrase seems to denote the personal presence of Christ with his saints in human nature, like, though different from, that in the time of his humiliation; then he dwelt or Tabernacle with men on earth, but it was in the form of a servant; but now he will appear in a glorious body, and indeed in all his personal glory, and reign among them as their King: . . . and he will dwell with them; in person and not by his Spirit, or by faith, as before, nor as a wayfaring man only for a night; but he will dwell with them for the space of a thousand years, and after that forever: Christ and his church will now be come together as husband and wife: and they shall be his people; that is, they shall appear to be his covenant people, that will be out of all doubt; this is made manifest in some measure in the effectual calling; but it does not yet appear neither to the saints themselves, nor to others, what they are, and shall be, but now it will be evident and unquestionable. And God himself shall be with them; the "Immanuel," God with us; . . . he himself will descend from heaven, when his church, the new Jerusalem does; the Lord their God will come in person with all the saints, and will be King over all the earth. And be their God, as Thomas styles him, my Lord, and my God." *John Gill Exposition of the New Testament.*

The Word Made Flesh

John 1:1 In the beginning was the Word, and the Word was with God, and the Word was God.

The Jewish Tabernacle, Temple, and Altars were worshipped facing East while the first Byzantine Church buildings, the worshippers facedWest.

Before the Entrance.

The Curtain/Posts of the Four Gospels
The Four Posts – Mathew, Mark, Luke, and John.
The Posts support the tri-colored curtain. Father – Son – Holy Spirit

The Outer Court – Place of Judgments and Sacrifice and Cleansing.
The Entrance Gate – The Word Became Flesh.

The Gate clearly marked as the one way a sinner or priest could access the outer court of God's house.
When the typical Israelite approached the Tabernacle, he found a wall of white linen around the entire Tabernacle area. That formed a barrier against him all the way around for 300-ft. by 450-ft., except for one stretch of 20 cubits, or 30-ft.

The Entrance Gate is formed only of white linen, but it was multi-colored in woven white, blue, purple, and red, and the curtains hung on four strong pillars.
The Entrance Gate is marked as the only way a sinner could access the court of God's house. This 30-**ft** Gate was the only entrance. Once an Israelite entered the Gate into the outer court with his sacrifice, he stood on "holy ground."

The Entrance Gate is 20-ft. by 30-ft. It was a curtain or screen made of richly woven material.

Exodus 27:16 For the Gate of the court there shall be a screen twenty cubits long, woven of blue, purple, and scarlet thread, and fine woven linen, made by a weaver. It shall have four pillars and four sockets.

*** There were no cherubim represented on this outdoor screen. The Cherubim are only visible within the Holy Place.

The Entrance Gate Screen with its blend of white, blue, purple, and scarlet, was identical to that hanging at the entrance to the Tabernacle building. However, it differed greatly from the white linen fence around the courtyard.

Please think of the beauty that would meet the eye of the Israelite as he approached the Gate of the Tabernacle. The sun's bright rays would be shining upon the four colors of the East Gate.

It is the single entrance to the entire Tabernacle. There is no other way the priest would carry out his duties or a repentant sinner seeking forgiveness, and a man had to enter by that one way. No one could enter by any other way except this Gate.

The massive curtain is 5ft. by 71/2ft. High and enclosed the outer court.

Any Israelite approaching the Tabernacle leading his sacrifice and desiring atonement knew there was no way to reach the bronze altar but through the East Gate that always faced East.

The Entrance Gate is always open. The Gate is never barred to forbid any person who wants to worship God.

However, one must make a personal decision to enter – if he is to receive an entry.

The Entrance Gate – The Type of Christ.

Jesus revealed Himself as the only entrance to God. The Eastern Gate of the Temple pointed to Him.

The righteousness of God bars every other way, but because of the blood of Christ, we have a way of approaching God. The tribe of Judah camped outside the Eastern Gate, the kingly tribe, and the tribe that means praise. Jesus sits as king with everything under Him. He is Malachi–Yahweh *[The Lord our King.]*

The worship of countless hosts will be unto Him for eternity*The Entrance Gate* reveals how beautiful Jesus is to behold. He is the altogether lovely One. In Him, there are no flaws. He is perfect in character. If we could see His face, we would see a look of love that would give us strength forever.

www.bible-history.com/Tabernacle/tab4the_entrance_Gate.htm.-of– the-shekel

John 14:6 Jesus saith unto him, I am the way, the truth, and the life: no man cometh unto the Father, but by me. Psa. 2:28–29; Isa. 44:6; Rev. 5:11–13.

The Entrance Gate's symbolism.

A. *The Entrance Gate* shows how to have access to God – The tearing of the Veil of the Holy of Holies.

> *Matt. 27:51 And, behold, the veil of the temple was rent in twain from the top to the bottom and the earth did quake, and the rocks rent.*
> *Matt. 27:50 Jesus, when he had cried again with a loud voice, yielded up the ghost.*

B. *The Entrance Gate* is the Representation of the True Tabernacle in Heaven. There is a real Tabernacle in the third Heaven, and Christ appeared before the throne of heaven as the Lamb of God.

> *Hebrews 9:11 But Christ being come an high priest of good things to come, by a greater and more perfect Tabernacle, not made with hands not of this building;*

**We, as the body of Christ dwells with each person, God does not dwell in a building, but within His people.

> *1 Cor. 6:19 What? know ye not that your body is the temple of the Holy Ghost which is in you, which ye have of God, and ye are not your own?*
> *Rev. 21:22 And I saw no temple [ναός is the O.T. Mishkan] therein: for the Lord God Almighty and the Lamb are the temple of it.*

C. *The Entrance Gate* ". . . when a common Israelite approached the Tabernacle, he found a wall of white linen around the entire Tabernacle formed a barrier against him around the Tabernacle for 300 cubits or 450-ft., except for one that stretched 20 cubits or 30-ft. and which was of a different fabric.

> "Once an Israelite entered the Gate into the outer court with his sacrifice, he was standing on "holy ground" *www.bible history.com/Tabernacle/*
> *Exodus 27:16 And for the Gate of the court shall be an hanging of twenty cubits, of blue, and purple, and scarlet, and fine twined linen, wrought with needle work and their pillars shall be four, and their sockets four.*
> Matthew, Mark, Luke, and John.

There were no cherubim represented on this outdoor screen. The Cherubim are only visible within the Holy Place and Holy of Holies' curtains. This screen, with its blend of white, blue, purple, and scarlet, was identical to that hanging at the entrance to the Tabernacle building. However, it was very different from the white linen fence around the entire courtyard. Please think of the beauty that would meet the eye of the Israelite as he approached the Gate of the Tabernacle.

d. It was the single entrance to the entire Tabernacle. There was no other way in; whether he was a priest going to carry out his duties or a repentant sinner seeking forgiveness, a man had to enter by that one way. No one could enter by any other way except this Gate. Any Israelite approaching the Tabernacle leading his sacrifice and desiring atonement knew that there was no way to reach the Bronze Altar but through the Gate that faced east." *Edited from Bible History.*

The Entrance Curtain – The Only Opening in the Fence.

The curtain of fine twined linen embroidered with blue, purple, and scarlet.

1. BLUE – Heavenly origin, nature – Son of God
2. PURPLE – Royalty – MATTHEW – The King of the Jews.
3. SCARLET – Sacrifice, death – MARK – The Suffering Servant.
4. LINEN – Righteousness – LUKE – The Perfect Son of Man.

The Entrance Gate was always open, never barred, with anyone to forbid a person who wanted to bring God the sacrifice for sin. However, one must make a personal decision to enter if he is to rec.

The Three Entrances – The Gate of the Courty – The Door to the Holy Place, The Veil to Holy of Holies.

1. GATE – Downward from God.
2. DOOR – Outward from God to man.
3. VEIL – Upward from man to God.
4. Gate 5ft x 20ft.; Door, Veil – 10ft x 10ft.
5. EXTRA WIDE – WHOSOEVER WILL.

The Significance of the Gate.

1. It was an ONLY GATE – One way Acts 4:12.
2. It was a WIDE GATE – "Whosoever will" Romans. 10:13.

3. It was an ACCESSIBLE GATE – No locks, no bars, with no cherubim seen.
4. It was an ATTRACTIVE GATE – A beautiful blend of colors.

https://bibleask.org/significance-city-Gate-naturally-spiritually

The Tabernacle's Structures.

1. Four Posts of Four Gospels and Four Curtains.
2. Four Posts – Matthew, Mark, Luke, and John.
3. Four Gospels – Support a tri-colored curtain. Father – Son – Holy Spirit.
4. Four coverings of the Tabernacle – First cover – curtain – Exodus 36:8–13.

The Most Holy Place – John 20:17 – The Place of God's Presence.

> *Hebrews 10:19–20 Having therefore, brethren, boldness, boldness:* [or, liberty] *to Enter into the holiest by the blood of Jesus. By a new and living way consecrated or newly made. for us, through the veil, that is to say, his flesh.*

John begins his gospel by telling us of Jesus, both creating Heaven and Earth.
John 1:1 In the beginning was the Word, and the Word was with God, and the Word was God.

– εν αρχη – The lack of a definite article shows the quality of event called "beginning."
– The noun emphasizes the character, nature, essence, or quality of a person or thing.
– See Wallace, Daniel. *Greek Grammar – Beyond the Basics*, 208, 209.
– was – ἦν – *Imperfect – A past action or state which is incomplete.*
– "λόγος" Is, first of all, a collecting or collection both of things in the mind, and of words by which they are expressed." *Robertson's Word Pictures StudyLight.org*
– λόγος – Usually, the written Word appears in 37 verses.
– ῥῆμα is the application of the λόγος "that which is or has been uttered by the living voice the spoken word."

Thayer's Greek Lexicon www.biblestudytools.com/lexicons/greek.

– "ῥῆμα" – The word occurs in 12 verses of John's Gospel.
– "of all time and created existence."

Jamieson, Fausset, and Brown www.blueletterbible.org/Comm/jfb/Jhn/Jhn_000.cfm

– "and the Word was (d) with God," "This word "with" points out that there is a distinction of persons here." *www.studylight.org/commentaries/eng/gsb/john-1.htm.*
– Lightfoot says, "These verses John 1:1– 18. give the key to understanding this Gospel.

StudyLight.org · https://www.studylight.org › eng › jlc

– "We have already said that the Son of God is thus placed above the world and above all the creatures." *Calvin's Commentaries – biblehub.com*

John 1:2 The <u>same</u> was in the beginning <u>with</u> the. God.

- same – οὗτος – "This one" previously mentioned.
- with – πρὸς – towards – face–to–face

John 1:3 <u>All</u> <u>things</u> were made by him; and without him was not anything made that was made.
And his coming down to this Earth. He explains, *"The Word became flesh and made his dwelling among us."*

Jesus went further when He chose to live among us. The God of the universe moved into this creation and was not recognized. [vs. 10] God stepped down as a man into a little town in Israel. He had to deal with sunburn, acne, and hunger. He knew what it was like to laugh with His best friends. He suffered through homelessness, going to Egypt, physical pain, and experiencing the joys, pains, sorrows, and limitations of being human. We can find hope in whatever we are going through. there is a personal God that loves you and can honestly say, "I've been there too." God is not merely above us or beyond us; He is with us. "When people entered the Tabernacle, they were facing west – in opposition to the pagan sun worshippers of the day who always faced east."

- All things – πάντα – Every individual thing.
- were made – ἐγένετο – Aorist – *This is a punctiliar point-in-time activity.*
- "Creation is thus presented as a becoming."
  Robertson's Word Pictures – scripturespeaks.org
- by – διά – through him

John 1:4 In him was <u>life</u>; and the life was the light of men.

- life – ζωὴ means "existence as contrasted with death."
  Vincent's Word Studies https://biblehub.com/commentaries/vws/john/1.htm.

John 1:5 And the light shineth in darkness; and the darkness <u>comprehended</u> it not.

- shineth – is shining and is still shining. *Present – This is an ongoing activity in the present time of the speaker.*
- comprehended – κατέλαβεν – grasped or seized.
- "John's thought is that in the struggle between light and darkness, light was victorious."
  Vincent's Word Studies biblehub.com/commentaries/vws/john/1.htm.

John 1:6 – 28 The Messenger

- Remember that John is a Levite Priest. John's father is a Levitical priest over the course of Abija Abijah, and his mother directly relates to Aaron, the High Priest.

Numbers 8:5– 2, Moses inducted the Levites into Tabernacle's service, including the sprinkling of them with the ashes of the Red Heifer. Levi had three sons, Gershon, Kehot, and Merari. When transporting the Tabernacle, each clan had different duties. "The Kehot would transport the Holy Ark, and other accouterments and the Gershon carried the curtains, the Merari carried the beams and bars." "The Levites were divided into 24 <u>mishmarot</u> [guards] each group served one week in the Tabernacle before relinquishing their place to the next Mishmar in the roster."

www.sefaria.org. www.chabad.org/library/article

A. John, not the Apostle is baptizing in Bethany across the Jordan River Valley.
   Luke 3:1 Now in the fifteenth year of the reign of Tiberius Caesar 29 AD.
   Luke 3:2 Annas and Caiaphas being the high priests, the word of God came unto John the son of Zacharias, in the wilderness.
B. John the Baptist is identified as the prophet Elijah. Matthew 1:7– 14.
C. Flavius Josephus in *Antiquities of the Jews 18.5.2.* mentions John the Baptist.
D. Josephus gives a public reason for this act of Herod Antipas, the fear that John would "raise a rebellion."
E. John's relationship with Jesus is through their mother.

John 1:6 There was a man sent <u>from</u> God, whose name was John.

- from – παρὰ – From beside God.
- John the Baptist was sent with a message.

John 1:7 The <u>same</u> came for a witness, to bear witness of the Light, <u>that</u> <u>all</u> men through him <u>might</u> believe.

- same – οὗτος – "This one" The one previously mentioned.
- for – εἰς – into – to
- ἵνα – in-order-that.
- all men – πάντες – everyone – every individual.
- might believe – πιστεύσωσι – *Aorist Subj. – Hypothetical situations.*

John 1:8 John the Baptist. He was not that Light but was sent <u>to</u> bear witness <u>of</u> that Light.

- to – ἵνα – in-order-that
- of – περὶ – around, about

John 1:9 That was the true <u>Light</u>, which <u>lighteth</u> every man that <u>cometh</u> into the world

- lighteth – φωτίζει – is lighting – *Present – This is an ongoing activity in the present time of the speaker.*
- cometh – ἐρχόμενον – "every man as he comes into the world." The Light is coming. *Present Participle – This is an ongoing activity in the present time of the speaker.*

John 1:10 He was <u>in</u> the <u>world</u>, and the world was made by him, and the world knew him not.

- in – ἐν – even before he arrives in Bethlehem
- world – κόσμος – the ordered world, not the planet, but society.
- His stay was temporary. One day, Jesus' stay will be permanent.

John 1:11 He <u>came</u> unto his <u>own</u>, and his <u>own</u> received him not.

- came – ἦλθε – *Aorist – This is a punctiliar point-in-time activity.*
- his own – things – ἴδια – The word is neuter.
- his own people. [Judeans] The noun is masculine.
- Jews refer to the "[Judeans]" or" the leaders in Judea.
- *Romans 1:1 I say then, Hath God cast away his people? God forbid.*
- *Romans 1:5...this present time also there is a remnant according to the election of grace.*

John 1:12 But as many of the [Judeans] as received him, to them gave he <u>power</u> to become the <u>sons</u> of God, even to them that believe <u>on</u> into. his name:

- power – ἐξουσίαν – authority
- sons – τέκνα – *The* result of being born from above – 3:16.
- on – εἰς – into

John 1:13 Which were born, not of blood, nor of the <u>will</u> of the flesh, nor of the will of man, but of God.

- will – θελήματος – The desirous will of God.
- of – ἐκ – out of – The source of new birth.

John 1:14 And the Word was made flesh, and dwelt among us, and we beheld his glory. [Shekinah?] the glory as of the only begotten of the Father, full of grace and truth.

- was made – ἐγένετο – *Aorist Mid. – A point-in-time activity for themselves,*
- "He entered into a new mode of being, not a new being."
  www.studylight.org/commentaries/eng/vnt/john.html.
- dwelt – ἐσκήνωσεν – Tabernacled – *Aorist Mid.– A point-in-time activity fo themselves.*
- among us – "as in a tent"
- "of the same material as a man."
- we – Peter, James, and John at Mt. of Transfiguration. See John 17:24.
- among – ἐν – usually translated as "in" our midst.
- "He came from glory – to bring us to glory." Hebrews 2:10.
  A. W. Tozer https://www.sermonindex.net/modules/articles/index

John 1:15 John bare witness of him, and cried saying, this is he of whom I spake He that cometh after me is preferred before me: for he was before me.

- bare– – bearing – *Present – This is a ongoing activity in the present time of the speaker.*
- μαρτυρεῖ – To affirm that one has seen or heard.
- cried – κέκραγε – *Perfect Tense – A completed action with continuing effects.*
- after me – ὀπίσω μου – i.e., Behind me in time.
- before me – πρῶτος – First in time.
  "That is, "He before whom I am sent to prepare him the way": so that these words refer to the time of his calling, and not of his age, for John was six months older than Christ." *www.studylight.org/commentaries/eng/gsb/john-1.htm.l*
- because – ὅτι – because of

John 1:16 And out of his fulness have all we received, and grace for grace.

- out of – ἐκ – "all the attributes of God summed up in Christ."
  Robertson's Word Pictures www.scripturespeaks.org/verse/John
- grace for grace – Like manna, we need the living Bread new every morning.

John 1:17 For because of the law was given by Moses, but grace and truth came by Jesus Christ.

- by – διὰ – through – Only truth came through Moses and Jesus.

Rodney F. Price, D.Min.

John 1:18 No man <u>hath</u> <u>seen</u> God at any time; the only begotten <u>Son</u>, which is <u>in</u> the bosom of the Father, he hath declared him.

- seen – ever seen – ἐώρακε – *Perfect – A completed action with continuing effects.*
- only begotten – μονογενὴς – He is not a created Son.
- Son – υἱὸς – He is positioned as a legal Son, not a natural son.
- in – into – εις
- in the bosom of the Father – "A remarkable expression, used only here, presupposing the Son's conscious existence distinct from the Father, and expressing His immediate and most endeared access to, and absolute acquaintance with, Him."
  Jamieson, Fausset, and Brown www.blueletterbible.org/Comm/jfb/Jhn/Jhn_000.cfm.

The Testimony of John the Baptist.
John 1:19 And this is the <u>record</u> of John, when the <u>Jews</u> [Judean leaders.] sent and Levites from Jerusalem to ask him, Who art thou?

- a record – μαρτυρία – testifying
- Jews – Ἰουδαῖοι – 1st mention of the leaders of the Sanhedrin.
- priests – ἱερεῖς – Who offered the sacrifices.
- The Sadducees and Levites served in all the Temple services.

John 1:20 And he confessed and denied not; but confessed, I am not the Christ.

- According to *Vincent's Studies,* this is John's combination of a positive/negative clauses.
  Vincent's Word Studies www.studylight.org/commentaries/eng/vnt/john.html,
- How many had false "Christs" appeared in Israel?

John 1:21 And they asked him, What then? Art thou Elias? And he saith, I am not. Art thou that prophet? And he answered, No.

- "Jesus only asserts that John was Elijah in spirit. They had just seen Elijah on the Mount of Transfiguration." Mark 19:4 *ccel.org/ccel/robertson_at/word.vii.i.html.*

John 1:22 Then said they unto him, Who art thou? that we may give an answer to them that sent us. What sayest thou of thyself?

- This is the same question as at first in John 1:19.

- "they might be capable of giving an account of him to the Sanhedrin.
John Gill Exposition of the New Testament.

John 1:23 He said, I am the [a] voice of one crying in the wilderness, Make <u>straight</u> the way of the Lord, as said the prophet Esaias.

- a. – The indefinite article is absent in Greek documents.
- straight – εὐθύνατε – "make straight, level, plain."
Thayer's Greek Lexicon www.biblestudytools.com/lexicons/greek.
- John quotes Isa. 40:3.

John 1:24 And they a second group? which were sent were of the <u>Pharisees</u>.

- The group which opposed Antiochus VI Epiphanes. King of Syria; 175-164. B.C.
- Pharisees – Josephus says that 6,000 existed at this time.
- The Pharisees of Acts 26: are active during the Second Temple period 515 BC-70 AD.
  They followed the Oral Law in addition to the Torah and attempted to live in a constant state of purity.
- Pharisees are distinguished by strict observance of the traditional and written law and are commonly held to have pretensions to superior sanctity.
- "The Sadducees did not believe that man would experience resurrection after physical eath. The Pharisees believed that God would send the Jews, a Messiah who would bring peace to the world and rule from Jerusalem."
Who were the Sadducees? | GotQuestions.org.
- "The lives of Jews were "divinely ordained."   *www.differencebetween.net*

John 1:25 And they asked him, and said unto him, Why <u>baptizest</u> thou then, <u>if</u> thou be not that Christ, nor Elias, neither that prophet?

- asked – *Aorist Middle – A point-in-time activity.*
- baptizes – Jewish baptism was usually self–administered.
- if – εἰ – *1ˢᵗ class condition – assumes reality.*

John 1:26 John answered them, saying, I baptize with in. water: but there <u>standeth</u> one <u>among</u> you, whom ye <u>know</u> not;

- among – μέσος – *Perfect Tense – A completed action with continuing effects.*
- Was Jesus standing in the group of Pharisees?

- in – ἐν – "a primary preposition denoting a fixed position – in place."
- know – οἴδατ – To know intellectually.

Thayer's Greek Lexicon www.biblestudytools.com/lexicons/greek.

John 1:27 He it is, who coming after me is preferred before me, whose shoe's latchet I am not worthy <u>to</u> unloose.

- to – ἵνα - in-order-that I should.

John 1:28 These things were done in <u>Bethabara</u> beyond Jordan, where John was baptizing.

- Bethabara – "House of the ford."
- Bethany – Βηθανία – was baptizing – *Present Part.* – *This is an ongoing activity in the present time of the speaker.*
- This is not the same place as the Bethany of John 1:18.

John 1:29 The next day <u>John</u> <u>seeth</u> Jesus <u>coming</u> unto <u>towards</u> him and saith, <u>Behold</u> the Lamb of God, which <u>taketh</u> away the <u>sin</u> of the world.

- John – Remember that John is a Levite.
- next day – *2ⁿᵈ day.*
- seeth – *Present Middle* – *This is an ongoing activity in the present time of the speaker.*
- towards – πρὸς
- Behold – ἴδε – Imperative command.
- taketh away – *Present Part.* – *This is an ongoing activity in the time of the speaker.*
- sin – ἁμαρτία – What sin?
- When ἁμαρτία is singular, it may refer to the sin nature.
- Occurs at the Passover for the sin of Israel.
- Jesus as the Lamb of God and for the world, not just for Jews.

John 1:30 This is he of whom I said, After me <u>cometh</u> a man which is preferred <u>before</u> me: for he was <u>before</u> me.

- cometh – ἔρχεται – *Present Middle* – he is coming for himself.
- before – ἔμπροσθέν – In front of me.
- before – πρῶτός – First in time or place.

John 1:31 And I <u>knew</u> him not: but that he should be made manifest to <u>Israel</u> therefore am I come baptizing with in. water.

- knew – ἤδειν – "to perceive with the eyes." *Thayer's Greek Lexicon*
  https://www.biblestudytools.com/lexicons/greek
- Israel – Southern Kingdom
- John did not know Jesus as the Messiah before this event.

John 1:32 And John <u>bare</u> <u>record</u>, saying, I <u>saw</u> the Spirit <u>descending</u> from out of. Heaven <u>like</u> a dove, and it abode upon him.

- bare record – ἐμαρτύρησεν – To be a witness – *Aorist Act. – A point in time activity.*
- saw – τεθέαμαι – *Perfect Tense – A completed action with continuing effects.*
- descending – καταβαῖνον – down from above. – *Present Part. – This is an ongoing activity in the present time of the speaker.*
- like – ὡς – as it were

John 1:33 And I <u>knew</u> him not: but he that sent me to baptize with water, the same one. said unto me, Upon whom thou shalt see the Spirit <u>descending</u> and <u>remainig</u> <u>on</u> him, the same is he which <u>baptizeth</u> <u>with</u> [in] the Holy Ghost.

- Knew – ἤδειν – by information
- descending - καταβαῖνον – down from – *Present Part. – This is an ongoing activity. in the present time of the speaker.*
- remaining – μένω – to remain, abide – *Present Act. Part. – This is an ongoing activity in the present time of the speaker.*
- on – ἐφ' – ἐπί – upon
- baptizeth – *Present Part. – This is a ongoing activity in the present time of the speaker.*

John 1:34 And I saw, and bare record that this is the <u>Son</u> of God.
The Lamb's first Disciples are from Judea.

- Son – υἰὸς – He is positioned as the legal son of God.

John 1:35 – 39 Jesus Calls Philip and Nathanael – the first Disciples.
John 1:35 Again the <u>next</u> <u>day</u> after John <u>stood</u> and <u>two</u> of his disciples;

- next day – 3rd day.
- stood – εἰστήκει – was standing – *Imperfect – A past action which is incomplete.*
- two – Of Jesus' disciples, Andrew and the Apostle John.

John 1:36 And <u>looking</u> upon Jesus as he <u>walked</u>, he saith, Behold the <u>Lamb of God</u>!

- looking – ἀμνός – look – ***Aorist*** *– This is a punctiliar point-in-time activity.*
- walked – περιπατοῦντι – walking about – *Present Part. – This is an ongoing activity in the present time of the speaker.*
- Lamb of God – "ο αμνος του θεου" – Rev. 2:1–3.

John 1:37 And the <u>two</u> disciples heard him speak, and they <u>followed</u> Jesus.

- two – Andrew and the Apostle John.
- Andrew – Ἀνδρέας – "manly."
- John – Ἰωάννης – "Jehovah is a gracious giver."
- followed – ἠκολούθησαν – *Aorist – This is a punctiliar point-in-time activity.*

John 1:38 Then Jesus turned, and saw them <u>following</u>, and saith unto them, What <u>seek</u> ye? They said unto him <u>Rabbi</u>, which is to say, being interpreted, <u>Master</u>, where <u>dwellest</u> thou?

- seek – ζητεῖτε – seeking – *Present – An ongoing activity in the present time of the speaker.*
- Rabbi – ῥαββί – a title
- Remember that Jesus is not trained in a Rabbinical School.
- Master – διδάσκαλε – A teacher.
- dwellest – μενεις – dwelling – *Present – This is an ongoing activity of the speaker.*

John 1:39 He saith unto them, Come and see. They came and saw where he dwelt, and abode with him that day: for it was about the <u>tenth</u> <u>hour</u>.

- tenth hour – Roman time – δεκάτη – 1 a.m.
- tenth hour – Jewish time – δεκάτη – 4 p.m.

Jesus' Galilean Ministry 28– 29 AD.
John 1:40 – 51; 2:1–12; 4:1–; 4:43–45; 6:1–14; 6:1 –21; 6:2 –71; 7:14.
John 1:40 – 42 The Third Disciple.

John 1:40 One of the two <u>which</u> <u>heard</u> John speak, and followed him, was Andrew, Simon Peter's brother.

- That heard from John. *Robertson's Word Pictures StudyLight.org*

John 1:41 He first <u>findeth</u> his own brother <u>Simon</u>, and saith unto him, We have <u>found</u> the Messias, which is, being interpreted, the Christ.

- findeth – εὑρίσκει – *Present – This is an ongoing activity in the present time of speaker.*
- Simon – Simon is his Aramaic name.
- Messiah is an Aramaic title, only here and in 4:25.
- found – εὑρήκαμεν – *Perfect Tense – **C**ompleted action with continuing effects.*
- "The first of the Eureka passages."

Vincent's Word Studies www.studylight.og/commentaries/eng/vnt/john.html.

- "We have found the Messias, which is, being interpreted, the (u) Christ…That is, anointed, and king after the manner of the Jewish people."
  1599 Geneva Bible-PD- www.studylight.org/commentaries/eng/gsb/john-1.htm.l

John 1:42 And he brought him to Jesus. And when Jesus beheld him, he said, Thou art Simon the son of Jona: thou shalt be called <u>Cephas</u>, which is by interpretation a <u>stone.</u>

- stone – Κηφᾶς – Cephas – a piece of rock – stone
- Πέτρος – A large piece of rock.

John 1:43-49 Jesus Calls Philip and Nathanael.
These verses are not directly related to the Tabernacle.

The Laver is a Place to see yourself.

John 2:1– 25 Jesus' Galilean Ministry 28 to 29 AD.

John 2:1 – 25 The Laver

The filling the Laver. The service of Levitical Priests of the first one chosen.

The Introduction to the three persons that need to be washed in water.

    John 3 – The Religious – Nicodemus

    John 4 – The Semi–religious – The Samaritan Woman

    John 5 – Those with a Crippled Faith – A Jew lacking any desire for a healing.

9

John 2:1 And the third day there was a marriage in <u>Cana</u> of Galilee; and the mother of Jesus was there:

- This is not Cana in Coelo–Syria.
- Place – Traveling on Tuesday from Bethany, 20 miles from Jerusalem.
- Ten days before the Passover.
- "Marriage festivals sometimes lasted a whole week."
           Vincent's Word Studies https://biblehub.com/commentaries/vws/john/2.htm.
- A wedding usually occurs one year after engagement.

- This town is the home of Nathanael.
- Was Mary related to this family?
- – Why is Joseph missing?

John 2:2 And both Jesus was called, and his disciples, to the <u>marriage</u>.

- marriage – The Example of Leah and Rachael.
- The marriage is usually one year after the engagement.
- 10 days before the Passover.

John 2:3 And when they <u>wanted</u> <u>wine</u>, the mother of Jesus saith unto him, They have no wine

- They wanted – υστερησαντος – to be in want of – *Aorist Act. Part. – A point-in-time* activity.
- The quests expected more wine and their expectations are not met.
- wine – οινου – not *γλυκόζη* – glucose – sugar water.
- "Due to the arrival of the seven guests."
  Robertson's Word Pictures www.studylight.org/commentaries/eng/rwp/john-2.htm.l

John 2:4 Jesus saith unto her, <u>Woman</u>, what have I to do with thee? <u>mine</u> <u>hour</u> is not yet come. – Woman – γυναι – This is a polite term for a married woman.

- Is she a widow?
- mine hour – The definite time of his death. See 7:30; 8:20; 2:23, 27; 13:1; 17:1.

John 2:5 His <u>mother</u> saith unto the <u>servants</u>, whatsoever he saithing unto you, do it.

- mother – μήτηρ – A natural relationship.
- servants – διακόνοις – Remember that deacons are simply servants.

John 2:6 And there were set there six <u>waterpots</u> <u>of stone,</u> after the manner of the <u>purifying</u> of the Jews, containing two or three firkins apiece.

- The six purification pots – 20/30 gallons of water.
- For the washing of hands before eating.
- purifying – καθαρισμὸν – Here and in Hebrews 1:3.
- 2 Kings 3:11; Mark 7:3.

John 2:7 Jesus saith unto them, Fill the <u>waterpots</u> with water. And they filled them up to the brim.

- These empty stone jars.

John 2:8 And he saith unto them, <u>Draw</u> out now, and bear unto the <u>governor</u> of the feast. And they bare it.

- Draw – ἀντλέω – First, To dip in the water. – *Aorist – This is a punctiliar point-in-time Activity.*
- governor – ἀρχιτρικλίνῳ – governor – The ruler of the feast.
- Ruler of the dining room who arranged the sitting couches and tasted the food.

John 2:9 When the <u>ruler</u> of the feast had <u>tasted</u> the water that was made wine, and <u>knew</u> not whence it was: the <u>governor</u> of the feast called the bridegroom,

- ruler – governor – ἀρχιτρίκλινος – The servants that drew the water knew.
- tasted – *Aorist – This is a punctiliar point-in-time activity.*

John 2:10 And saith unto him, Every man at the beginning doth set forth <u>good</u> <u>wine</u>; and when men have well drunk, then that which is worse: but thou hast kept the <u>good</u> <u>wine</u> until now.

- good – καλός – good – Intrinsically good.
  > *Vine's Greek N.T. Dictionary Expository Dictionary of Old and New Testament Words.*
- wine – οινος – This is not grape juice or sugar water.

John 2:11 This beginning of <u>miracles</u> did Jesus in Cana of Galilee, and manifested forth his glory; and his disciples believed on him.

- miracles – signs – σημεῖον – Signs only occur in John and not a miracle.
- Scripture has not a single word translated as a "miracle."
- The English word "miracle" comes from the Latin term "*miraculum*" which merely refers to something that evokes wonder.
- There are four primary Greek words translated as a miracle: works-ἔργον. wonders-τέρας, powers-δύναμις and signs-σημεῖον.

John 2:12 After this he went down to <u>Capernaum</u>, he, and his mother, and his brethren, and his Disciples: they continued there not many days.

- Capernaum on the north shore of Galilee.
- The hometown of the tax collector Matthew.

John 2:13– 17 The cleansing of the Temple.
John 2:13 And the Jews' <u>passover</u> was at hand, and Jesus went up to Jerusalem,

- Christ's first Passover.
- The Month of Nisan begins the Sacred calendar of the nation.

John 2:14 And found in the <u>temple</u> those that sold oxen and sheep and doves, and the changers of <u>sitting</u>.

- temple – ἱερῷ – Temple grounds, not the sanctuary, in the Court of the Gentiles.
- sitting – καθημενο – *Present Participle – An action that is currently taking place, and indicating a habit.*

John 2:15 And when he had made a scourge of small cords, he drove them all out of the <u>temple</u> and the sheep, and the oxen; and poured out the changers' <u>money</u>, and overthrew the tables;

- temple – ἱερόν – The Temple grounds.
- money – κερματιστής – Small coins are often changed to shekels into half shekels to buy ceremonially clean animals.

John 2:16 And said unto them that sold doves, <u>Take</u> these things hence; make not my Father's house an house of <u>merchandise</u>.

- Take – *Aorist Imperative – A point-in-time activity – command.*
- Merchandise – ἐμπορίου – A den of robbers.
- The Sadducees and Pharisees in the Sanhedrin approved their activity.
  A. T. Robertson's Word Pictures www.studylight.org/commentaries/eng/rwp/john.

John 2: 17 And his disciples remembered that it was written, The <u>zeal</u> of thine house hath eaten me up.

- Zeal – ζῆλος – The fervour of spirit. "Zeal" in this place is taken for a wrathful indignation and displeasure of the mind, brought about when someone deals. wickedly and evilly towards those whom we love well."
  https://biblehub.com/commentaries/john/1-20.htm.

John 2:18– 22.

John 2:18 Then answered the Jews and said unto him, What sign [σημεῖον] shewest thou unto us, seeing that thou doest these things?

- "These traders had paid the Sadducees and Pharisees in the Sanhedrin for the concession as traffickers which they enjoyed. They were within their technical rights in this question."
  A. T. Robertson's Word Pictures. *www.studylight.org/commentaries/eng/rwp/john.htm.*

John 2:19 Jesus answered and said unto them, Destroy this <u>temple</u>, and in three days I will raise it up.

- Not a reference to Herod's temple.
- Temple – ναός – The sacred edifice.
- vs. 21. Jesus' body is the Holy of Holies.
- The 3rd Temple is to be built by the Messiah.

John 2:20 Then said the Jews, Forty and six years was this <u>temple</u> and wilt thou rear it up in three days?

- temple – Herod's temple.
- Herod's temple not finished until 63 AD.
- "They were looking at the physical structure in Hebrew "Mikdash" of the temple, but He said, "Destroy this temple" He used the word in Hebrew "Mishkan" which was the word used in the Old Testament of the Presence that lit the Holy of Holies on Yom Kippur in the tabernacle or temple. Jesus said I am the temple Mishkan. of God. When the glory the "Sh'chinah" would come down like a tornado or funnel right through the roof of the Holy of holies and the Presence would on the mercy seat between the cherubim after the blood was sprinkled, that was the mishkan."
  www.bible– history.com/tabernacle.

John 2:21 But he spake of the <u>temple</u> of his body.

- temple – ναός – The sacred edifice.

John 2:22 When therefore he was risen from the dead, his disciples <u>remembered</u> that he had said this unto them; and they believed the scripture, and the word which Jesus had said.

- "they believed that the Scripture was true."

    Vincent's Word Studies https://biblehub.com/commentaries/vws/john/21.htm.

John 2:23 Now when he was in Jerusalem at in. the passover, in the <u>feast</u> <u>day</u>, man believed in his name, when they saw the <u>miracles</u> which <u>he</u> <u>did</u>.

- feast day – Feast of Unleavened Bread.
- miracles – σημεῖα – signs
- he did. – εποιει – *Imperfect – A past action or state which is incomplete.*

John 2:24 But Jesus did not <u>commit</u> himself unto them, because he <u>knew</u> all men.

- commit – ἐπίστευεν – to trust
- knew – γινώσκειν – To knew by experience. – *Present Infinitive – This is a ongoing activity in the present time of the speaker.*
- As a Pharisee, "he belonged to that party which with all its bigotry contained a salt true patriotism and could rear such cultured and high-toned man as Gamaliel and Paul

    A. T. Robertson www.studylight.org/commentaries/eng/rwp/john.html.

John 2:25 And needed not that any should testify of man: for he <u>knew</u> what was in man.

- knew – ἐγίνωσκε – *Imperfect – A past action or state which is incomplete.*

The Laver of Brass.

John 3:1– 36 The Laver

Nicodemus, the first person to be washed – The religious man.
The Necessity of Regeneration. Jesus' message of being born again in to even to
See the Kingdom of God must be Born Again.

John 3:1 There was a man of the <u>Pharisees</u>, named <u>Nicodemus</u>, a <u>ruler</u> of the Jews [Judeans]:

- Pharisees – Φαρισαῖος – The Jewish sectary of Sanhedrin.
- Nicodemus – His name means victorious among his people.
- ruler – The first in rank – chief

John 3:2 The same came to Jesus by night, and said unto him, <u>Rabbi</u>, we <u>know</u> that thou art teacher <u>come from</u> God: for no man can do these miracles that thou doest, <u>except</u> God be with him.

- Rabbi – An official title of honor.
- know – οἴδαμεν – Intellectual knowledge
- come from – οτι ἀπὸ – From the presence of God.

- except – ἐὰν – *3rd* class condition of assumed probability.
- we know – οἴδαμεν – as a group. "Assured conviction based on Jesus' miracles.
  Vincent's Word Studies https://biblehub.com/commentaries/vws/john/3.
- except – ἐὰν – *3rd class condition of assumed probability.*
- "Jesus means that something must first happen to a person described as being born anew/from above. Before the possibility of entering the Kingdom of God. Jesus elaborates that unless a person is born of water and the Spirit that he or she cannot enter the Kingdom of God."
  Jamieson, Fausset, and Brown www.blueletterbible.org/Comm/jfb/Jhn/Jhn_000.cfm.

John 3:3 Jesus answered and said unto him, Verily, verily, I say unto thee, <u>except</u> a man be <u>born again</u>, he cannot see the kingdom of God.

- except – ἐὰν – *3rd class condition of assumed probability.*
- born again – ἄνωθεν – from above – The source of the new birth is external.
- cannot – οὐ δύναται – He is without any added power.
- kingdom – βασιλείαν – God's personal rule is over people, and <u>not</u> over territory.

John 3:4 Nicodemus saith unto him, How can a man be born <u>when</u> <u>he</u> <u>is</u> <u>old</u>? can he enter the time into his mother's womb, and be <u>born</u>?

- when old? – γέρων – an old man – How "old" is Nicodemus?
- can he – μὴ δύναται – Nicodemus anticipates a negative answer.
- ". . . that Jews themselves should need a new birth was to him incomprehensible."
  Jamieson, Fausset, and Brown <u>www.blueletterbible.org/Comm/jfb/Jhn/Jhn_000.cfm</u>.

John 3:5 Jesus answered, Verily, verily, I say unto thee, <u>Except</u> a man be <u>born</u> <u>of</u> out of <u>water</u> and of the [a] Spirit, he cannot enter into the kingdom of God.

- except – ἐξ ὕδατος – ἐὰν – *3rd class condition of assumed probability.*
- of – ἐξ – out of
- water – Is Jesus referring to the baptism of repentance of John the Baptist?
- a – Remember there is not an indefinite article in the Greek text.
- It is intended to explain the meaning of being born anew/from above.
- Being born of water and the Spirit probably refers to the ongoing ministry of John the Baptist's baptism of repentance and the baptism of the Spirit.

John 3:6 – 13 The Manner of New Birth, the Work of the Holy Spirit.
John 3:6 That which is out. of the flesh is flesh, and that which is born out of of the is spirit.

- γεγεννημένον – *Perfect Pass. Part. – A completed action with continuing effects.*
- *Ezek. 36:25 – 27 Then will I sprinkle clean water upon you, and ye shall be clean from all your filthiness, and from all your idols, will I cleanse you. A new heart also will I give you, and a new spirit will I put within you: and I will take away the stony heart out of your flesh, and I will give you an heart of flesh. And I will put my spirit within you, and cause you to walk in my statutes, and ye shall keep my judgments, and do them.*
- *Titus 3:5 - Not by works of righteousness which we have done, but according to his mercy he saved us, by the washing of regeneration, and renewing of the Holy Ghost.*

John 3:7 <u>Marvel</u> not that I said unto thee, <u>Ye</u> <u>must</u> be born <u>again</u>.

- Marvel – θαυμάσῃς – *Aorist Subjunctive – A punctiliar point-in-time of a possible acivity.*
- Ye – ὑμᾶς – plural, therefore, as a group of people, not just Nicodemus.
- must – necessary *(as* binding*)*
- born again – ἄνωθεν – from above

John 3:8 The <u>wind</u> bloweth where it <u>listeth</u> and thou hearest the sound thereof, but canst not tell it cometh, and whither it goeth: so is every one that is born out <u>of</u> the Spirit.

- wind – πνευμα – spirit – πνεύματος.
- <u>listeth</u> – θελει – to desire – The cause of the new birth is not by any human effort.
- of – ἐκ – out of

John 3:9 Nicodemus answered and said unto him, How can these <u>things</u> be?

- things – Concerning the process of being born again.

John 3:10 Jesus answered and said unto him, Art thou a <u>master</u> of Israel, and <u>knowest</u> not these things?

- master – διδάσκαλος – teacher, instructor
- knowest – γινώσκεις – To know via experience.

John 3:11 Verily, verily, I say unto thee, <u>We</u> speak that we do <u>know</u>, and testify that we have seen; and ye receive not our witness.

- know – οἴδαμεν – Factual knowledge.
- we – Jesus and John the Baptist.
- ye – plural, as a group.
- "(i) You handle doubtful things even though you have no solid basis for believing them, and yet men believe you: but I teach those things that are of a truth and well known, and you do not believe me."

  https://www.studylight.org/commentaries/eng/gsb/john-3.html.

John 3:12 <u>If</u> I have told you earthly things, and ye believe not, how shall ye believe, <u>if</u> I tell you of heavenly things?

- if – εἰ – Is a 1st class condition – The speaker assumes a present reality.
- if – ἐὰν – Is a 3rd class condition assumes a "Future more probable condition."

John 3:13 And no man hath ascended up to heaven, but he that came down from heaven, even the <u>Son</u> of <u>man</u> which is in heaven.

- Son – υἱὸς – To be positioned as a son.
- man – ανθρωπουν – This word is used of man/mankind.
- Compare with John 1:18.

John 3:14– 17 The Means of New Birth – Condition of New Birth.
John 3:14 And as Moses lifted up the serpent in the wilderness, even so <u>must</u> the <u>Son of man</u> be lifted up: See Numbers 21.

- must – δεῖ – It is necessary as binding.
- Son of man – τον υιον του ανθρωπου
- "The reference here is to the crucifixion, but beyond that, to the glorification of Christ."
  Vincent's Word Studies https://biblehub.com/commentaries/vws/john/21.htm.

John 3:15 That whosoever believeth in him should not perish, but have <u>eternal</u> life.

- ἐκ – out of
- eternal – In John, eternal refers to the age of ages.
- eternal – αἰώνιον, aiōnios occurs with ζωὴν.

John 3:16 For God so <u>loved</u> the world, that he gave his only begotten Son, that whosoever believeth in him should not perish, but have everlasting life.

- loved – ἠγάπησεν – A relationship love.
- God maintains a relationship with humankind despite of their rebellion against him.

John 3:17 For God sent not his Son into the world to condemn the world; but <u>that</u> the world through him might be saved.

- that – ἵνα – in-order-that

John 3:18– 21 The Hindrance of New Birth is the Natural Man.
John 3:18 He that believeth on him is not condemned: but he that believeth not is condemned already, because he hath not believed in the name of the only begotten Son of God.

- condemned already – κρίνεται – *Perfect Pass. Part. – A completed action with continuing effects of krinō.*
- – "Judgment has already been passed on the one who refuses to believe in Christ as the Saviour sent by the Father, the man who is not willing to come to Christ for life."
  John Gill https://alkitab.sabda.org/commentary.
- ". . .from the beginning"; he remains under the sentence of condemnation passed in Adam upon him;" *John Gill https://alkitab.sabda.org/commentary.*

John, the Baptist, Exalts Christ.
John 3:19 And this is the <u>condemnation</u>, <u>that</u> light is <u>come</u> into the world, and men loved darkness rather than light, because their deeds were <u>evil</u>.

- condemnation – κρίσις – The process of judging.
- that – ὅτι – because
- come – ἐλήλυ – A permanent result – *Perfect Tense – A completed action with continuing effects.*
- evil – πονηρὰ – a malignant evil – pornea.

John 3:20 For every one that <u>doeth</u> <u>evil</u> hateth the light, neither cometh to the light, lest his deeds should be reproved.

- doeth – πράσσων – *Present Participle – An action that is currently taking place, and indicating a habit.*

- evil – φαῦλα – practice evil, slight, trivial
- "Every man, the series of whose life and conversation is vile, hates Christ and his Gospel, cause they make manifest his evil deeds, convict of them, and rebuke him for them." *Gill's Exposition 3:20 (biblehub.com)*
- Compare Eph. 5:11– 13.

John 3:21 But he that <u>doeth</u> truth cometh to the light, that his deeds may be made manifest that they are <u>wrought</u> in God.

- doeth – ποιῶν – doing – *Present Participle, An action that is currently taking place, and indicating a habit.*
- wrought – εἰργασμένα – working – *Perfect – Completed action with continuing effects.*

The Laver

John 4: The Woman of Samaria to be washed. – The semi-religious woman.
The Jesus' message concerning the everlasting life.

- Jesus sits at the well in Samaria.
- Samaria means "watch mountain" and is the name of both a city and a territory.

    When the Israelites conquered the Promised Land, this region they allotted to the tribes of Manasseh and Ephraim. The city of Samaria founded by King Omri around 880 BC. And is the capital of the northern kingdom of Israel.

    https://ttb.org/docs/default-source/notesnes/no23micah.pdf?sfvrsn=13791c16_2. The Samaritans argued that they were descendants of Joseph through his sons Manasseh and Ephraim. They also believed the center of worship should remain at Shechem, on Mount Gerizim, since the time of Joshua.

    Where they still sacrifice and worship.

    The Jews, however, built their first temple at Jerusalem. The Samaritans furthered the rift by producing their version of the Pentateuch, the five books of Moses. King Ahab built a temple to the pagan god Baal at that location. Jesus

    Included this city/territory in the Great Commission of the disciple's ministry. "There is a story in John 4 that occurs after Jesus travels some thirty hours out of his way to meet up with a Samaritan woman getting water in the middle of the day. We know she purposely avoids people because no one in their right mind would be out there at that hour in the middle of the desert. This woman found herself at the end of her rope. She is shunned by society, broken-hearted, and living a life of isolation. Jesus casually asks for some water. No, He did not travel for nearly two days for a drink. Jesus wanted to reveal a life-changing truth to this woman.And he explains that He offers "living water," See *John 4:10*.

This is the kind of encouragement that never goes away; it is a well that never runs dry. "The woman said to Him, 'Sir, give me this water, so I will not be thirsty.'(John 4:15). Jesus extends the same invitation to you, too. He is inviting us into a life-giving relationship with Him.

Burnout happens when we are running on empty, but Jesus offers us a path towards fullness & fulfillment. Burnout can be a blessing when it brings us closer to the ultimate source of life: Jesus. Just like He did for the woman at the well, Jesus will greatly help us. We do not have to change our location for Jesus to change your situation.

Edited Unknown Source

Samaria means "watch mountain" and is the name of a city and a territory. When the Israelites conquered the Promised Land, this region is allotted to the tribes of Manasseh and Ephraim. The city of Samaria was founded by King Omri around 880 BC. Samaria is the capital of the northern kingdom of Israel.

https://ttb.org/docs/default-source/notes-outlines/no23_micah.pdf?

John 4:1-6 The Woman at Jacob's well – The Samaritans of Sychar.

Jesus' surprising conversation with a woman at the well. He violated the social customs of the day.

– She is unclean because she is both a Gentile/Jew and a woman.
– "Men are not allowed to be talking to women, except within their own families.
– "One who excessively converses with a woman causes evil to himself, neglects the study of Torah, and, in the end, inherits purgatory."

https://www.meaningfullife.com/chapter-one-text-ethics-of-our-fathers
Talmud – Mishna Avot.

– "Men repeatedly advised against associating with women, although this is usually because of man's lust rather than because of any short-coming in women." *https://wwwJewfaq.org/women.htm.*
– "It is the way of a woman to stay at home and it is the way of a man to go out into the marketplace." *Bereshit Rabbah John 8:1; cf. Taanit 23b.*

https://www.sefaria.org › ... › Bereishit Rabbah

- Based on the passage in Deut. 4:9, "teach them to thy sons."
- The rabbis declared women exempt from the commandment to learn the Law.
- "Indeed, It is foolishness to teach Torah to your daughter." *Babylonian Talmud.*
  www.chabad.org/dailystudy/talmud_cdo/aid/3109424/jewish/Talmud-Sotah-20.htm.

John 4:1 When therefore the Lord knew how the Pharisees had heard that Jesus made and baptized more disciples than John,

- knew γνω – γινώσκω – to know by experience.
- Jesus and John, the Baptist had only baptized the 12 to work with him. We do not have any record of how many John had baptized to follow him.
- The method Christ took was, he first made men disciples, and then baptized them; and the same he directed his apostles to, saying, "go and teach," or "disciple all nations, baptizing them." *Gill's Exposition biblehub.com.*

John 4:2 Though Jesus himself baptized not, but his disciples.

- The correction by the Apostle John.

John 4:3 He left Judaea and departed again into Galilee.

- He avoids the Pharisees and Jerusalem in Judea now until the end of his ministry.

John 4:4 And he must needs go through Samaria.

- It was only necessary to pass through Samaria in going directly north from Judea to Galilee." *Robertson's Word Pictures www.ccel.org/ccel/robertson_at/word.vii.iv.html.*
- "The Samaritans, a mixture by intermarriage of the Jews, left in the land with colonists from Babylon and other regions sent by Shalmaneser." 2 Ch. 30:6, 2Ch. 34:9.
  www.ccel.org/ccel/robertson_at/word.vii.iv.htm.l
- "Israel had many dealing with the Samaritans. The disciple went to the city to buy food, etc. Using the personal items of the Samaritans is forbidden from deriving benefit from a Jew, and he is prohibited from deriving benefit from Samaritans called the Kutim. because they are also Shabbat observers. One who takes a vow that deriving benefit from those who eat garlic on Shabbat night is forbidden to him is prohibited from deriving benefit from a Jew, and he is prohibited from benefiting from Samaritans." *www.sefaria.org/Nedarim.31a.*

John 4:5 Then cometh he <u>to</u> a city of Samaria, which is called <u>Sychar</u>, near to the parcel of ground that Jacob gave to his son Joseph.

- to – εἰς – into
- Sychar – שכר – "drunken"
- City now called Neapolis; same as "Sichem"– "Shechem." Genesis 33:19.

John 4:6 Now Jacob's well was there. Jesus, therefore, being wearied with his journey, sat thus on the well: and it was about the sixth hour noon.

- The well dug in about 2,000 years earlier – πηγα, – a well fed by a spring.
- The well is located at the base of Mt. Gerizim.

The initiation of the Good News.
John 4:7 There cometh a woman of <u>Samaria</u> to draw water: Jesus saith unto her, Give me to drink.

- Samaria – The country because the city is about two hours away.
- It appears that she is alone.

John 4:8 For his disciples were gone away unto the city <u>to buy</u> meat.

- buy meat – At the market. – ἀγοράζ, – agorázō – The marketplace is a place to buy meat/ food.

John 4:9 Then saith the <u>woman</u> of Samaria unto him, How is it that thou, being <u>a Jew</u> askest drink of me, which am a <u>woman</u> of Samaria? for the <u>Jews</u> for have no dealings with the Samaritans.

- woman – γυνή – John relates that she is a married woman.
- She also recognizes that he, a Jew from the tribe of Judah they have no dealings with the Samaritans. "Public discourses with a married woman are improper; however, this is a private discussion." *Revised-Edited www.myjewishlearning.com*
- The Disciples, however, are going to a Samaritan city for commercial reasons.
- A Jew – Ἰουδαῖ – The tribe of Judah is to have no dealings with the Samaritans.

John 4:10 Jesus answered and said unto her, If thou knewest; the gift of God, and who it is that saith to thee, Give me to drink; thou wouldest have asked of him, and he would have given thee living water.

- If – εἰ – *Introduces a 2ⁿᵈ class condition – is determined as unfulfilled.*

John 4:11 The woman saith unto him, Sir, thou hast nothing to draw with, and the well is deep: from whence then hast thou that living water?

- The dug well about 100 feet deep. *www.preceptaustin.org/john-4-commentary.*
- The living-running water is like a spring or well supplied by springs.
- living – ζῶν – see John 7:38 – lively, moving – υδωρ ζων.

John 4:12 Art thou greater than our father Jacob which gave us the well, and drank thereof himself, and his children, and his cattle?

- Art thou – συ μειζων ει – She is expecting a negative answer.
- Jesus ignores her question.

John 4:13 Jesus answered and said unto her, Whosoever drinketh of this water shall thirst again.

- Whosoever – πᾶς ὁ πίη
- drinketh – πινων – To keep on drinking. – *Present Participle – Action that is currently taking place and indicating a habit.*
- out – εκ – of this well of water.
- Jesus is pointing to the well.

John 4:14 But whosoever drinketh of the water that I shall give him shall never thirst; but the water that I shall give him shall be in him a well of water springing up into everlasting life.

- well – πηγὴ – a fountain, spring up.
- springing – αλλομενου – gush – leaping, spring up, bubbling up.
- everlasting – αιωνιον – perpetual

John 4:15 The woman saith unto him, Sir, give me this water, that I thirst not, neither come hither to draw.

- give – δός – giving – *Present Participle, Action that is currently taking place, and indicating a habit.*

John 4:16– 18 The inquisitive Jesus.
John 4:16 Jesus saith unto her, Go, call thy <u>husband</u> and come hither.

- husband – ἄνδρα – He is a married man.

John 4:17 The <u>woman</u> answered and said, I have no <u>husband</u>. Jesus said unto her, Thou hast well said, I have <u>no</u> <u>husband</u>.

- woman – γυνὴ – The term for a married woman.
- no husband – ἀνήρ – She is not married to this married man. Therefore, she lives in adultery.

John 4:18 For thou hast had five <u>husbands</u> and he whom thou now hast is not thy <u>husband</u> in that saidst thou truly.

- husband – ἀνήρ.
- Therefore, not thy lawful husband.
- Jesus' view of marriage. See Matt.19: Jesus' answer to Sadducees' question.

John 4:19 The woman saith unto him, Sir, I <u>perceive</u> that thou art a prophet.

- perceive – θεωρῶ – I am perceiving – *Present – This is an ongoing activity in the present time of the speaker.*

John 4:20 Our fathers worshipped in this <u>mountain</u> and ye say, that in Jerusalem is the place where men ought to worship.

- "On Gerizim, are proclaimed the blessings recorded in Deut. 28.
  https://www.preceptaustin.org/john-4-commentar
- The Samaritans kept this temple worship on this mountain and sacrificed.

John 4:21 Jesus saith unto her, Woman, believe me, the hour <u>cometh,</u> when ye shall neither in this <u>mountain</u> nor yet at Jerusalem on Mt Zion worship the Father.

- mountain – Mt. Gerizim with a Temple for worship.
- cometh – ἔρχεται – coming

John 4:22 <u>Ye</u> worship <u>ŏ</u> what. <u>ye</u> know'/ not what: we <u>know</u> what <u>we</u> worship: for salvation <u>is</u> of the <u>Jews</u>.

- Ye – Samaritans
- know – οιδαμεν – Intellectual knowledge
- is εκ – out of – from
- Jews – [Judeans]

John 4:23 But the hour cometh, and now is, when the true <u>worshippers</u> shall worship the Father in spirit and in truth: for the Father seeketh such to worship him.

- worshippers – προσκυνηταὶ – The term occurs only here in the New Testament.
- "The phrase in spirit and in truth describes the two essential characteristics of true worship." *Vincent's Word Studies www.sacred-texts.com/bib/cmt/vws/joh004.htm.*
- "This is what matters, not where." *Robertson's Word Pictures StudyLight.org*
- "seeking" – ζητει – *Present – An ongoing activity in the present time of the speaker.*
- worshippers – προσκυνέω – "in the NT by kneeling or prostration to do homage." *Thayer's Greek-English Lexicon www.biblestudytools.com/lexicons/greek*

John 4:24 The. God <u>is a</u> Spirit: and they that worship him <u>must</u> worship him in spirit and in truth.

- omit – "is a" does not occur. Without a definite article, it shows the quality.
- πνευμα ο θεος "God is spirit" and not "a" spirit.
- The phrase describes the nature of God, and not the personality of God.
- must – δει – "is necessary." *Thayer's Greek-English Lexicon www.biblestudytools.com/lexicons/greek*

John 4:2– 26 The Disclosing of Information.

John 4:25 The woman saith unto him, I know that Messias <u>cometh</u> which is called Christ: when he is <u>come</u>, he will tell us all things.

- is coming himself – ερχεται – *Present Mid. – This is an ongoing activity in the present time of the speaker.*
- is come – ελθη – [2]*Aorist Subj.* – ἔρχομαι. – *This is a punctiliar potential point-in-time activity.*

~ 34 ~

John 4:26 Jesus <u>saith</u> unto her, I that <u>speak</u> unto thee, I am he.

- speak – λαλῶν – *Present Participle – An action that is currently taking place, and indicating a habit.*
- *Exodus 3:14 And God said unto Moses, I am that I am.*

John 4:27– 30 The Woman's Testimony by word and by deed.
John 4:27 And upon this came his disciples, and marvelled that he <u>talked</u> with the a woman:yet no man said, What seekest thou? or, Why talkest thou with her?

- talked – *Imperfect – A past action or state which is incomplete.*
- They thought, "he was acting in a way beneath his dignity."
  www.ccel.org/ccel/robertson_at/word.vii.iv.html.
- There was a rabbinical precept: "Let no one talk with a woman in the street, no, not with his wife." *Neil Lightfoot Hor, Hebr. iii. 287*
  www.ccel.org/ccel/robertson_at/word.vii.iv.html.

John 4:28 The woman then left her <u>waterpot</u>, and went her way into the city, and saith to the men,

- The waterpots for purification.
- Women usually carry them upon the head or their shoulders.

John 4:29 Come, see a man, which told me all things that ever I did: is <u>not</u> <u>this</u> the Christ?

- not this – μήτι ἐστιν – The particle suggests a negative answer.
- She is the first evangelist to the Samaritans.

John 4:30 Then they <u>went</u> <u>out</u> of the city and came unto him.

- went out – εξηλθον – *Aorist – This is a punctiliar point-in-time activity.*
- The Jews were not this eager to see Jesus.
- The Samaritans rushed out to see him.
- The immediate results of sowing the seed – **By** her testimony.

John 4:31– 38 The disciple's inquiry.
John 4:31 In the mean while his disciples <u>prayed</u> him, saying, Master, eat.

- prayed – ηρωτων – "kept beseeching him." – *Imperfect – A past action or state which is incomplete.*

- ". . . his disciples prayed him, saying, master, eat; for they perceived a disinclination in him to food; and they knew that he was weary with his journey, and that it was the time of day and high time, that he had had some food; and therefore out of great respect to him, and in concern for his health and welfare."

John Gill Exposition 4:41 biblehub.com

John 4:32 But he said unto them, I have meat to eat that ye know not of.

- "They were destined to learn that the soul may be nourished in obeying the will of God." *F. B. Meyer www.studylight.org/commentaries/eng/fbm/john-4.html.*

John 4:33 Therefore said the disciples one to another, <u>Hath</u> any man brought him ought to eat?

- μή τις – A negative answer is expected.

John 4:34 Jesus saith unto them, My meat is to do the <u>will</u> of him that sent me, and to <u>finish</u> his work.

- will – a desire – θελημα
- finish – πελειώσω – accomplished – *Aorist Subj. – This is a punctiliar potential and a point-in-time activity.*

John 4:35 Say not ye, There are yet four months, and then cometh harvest? behold, I say unto you, Lift up your eyes, and look on the fields; for they are white already to harvest.

- "It was about the latter end of November, or the beginning of December, that Christ is in Samaria, Barley harvest, which began at that time."

Edited *newspaperormagazinearticle/1664en.html.*
https://canadianmysteries.ca/sites/robinson/archives/

John 4:36 And he that reapeth receiveth the wages, and gathereth fruit unto life eternal: that both he that soweth and he that reapeth may rejoice together.

- No waiting, but reaping the fruit immediately follows the sowing.
- Sower and Reaper may rejoice together.
- "The spiritual harvester can gather his harvest without waiting four months. Jesus is reaping a harvest right now by the conversion of this woman."

Robertson's Word Pictures www.el.org/ccel/robertson_at/word.vii.iv.html.

John 4:37 And herein is that saying true, One soweth, and <u>another</u> reapeth.

- another – ἄλλος – Another of the same sort of person.
- "herein" In this relationship.
- *Psalm 126:5 They that sow in tears shall reap in joy.*
- *Psalm 126:6 He that goeth forth and weepeth, bearing precious seed, shall doubtless come again with rejoicing, bringing his sheaves with him.*

John 4:38 I sent you to reap that whereon ye bestowed no labour: <u>other men</u> laboured, and ye are entered into their labours.

- other men – another – ἄλλος – "another of the same sort."
- ". . . the prophets sowed, and the apostles reaped." *John Gill*
                                             John Gill Exposition of the New Testament.
- their labours – John the Baptist and the O. T. prophets. See Hebrews 9:10.

John 4:39– 42 The response of the disciples.
John 4:39 And many of the Samaritans of that city <u>believed</u> on him for the saying of the woman, which <u>testified</u> He told me all that ever I did.

- believed – ἐπίστευσαν – *Aorist – This is a punctiliar point-in-time activity.*
- testified – μαρτυρέω – to bear record.

John 4:40 So when the Samaritans <u>were come</u> unto him, they besought him that he would tarry with them: and he abode there two days.

- were come – ἔρχομαι – *Present Mid. – This is an ongoing activity in the present time of the speaker.*
- "those who were not His own,"
                Jamieson, Fausset, and Brown www.blueletterbible.org/Comm/jfb/Jhn/Jhn_000.cfm.

John 4:41 And many more <u>believed</u> because of his own word;

- believed – επιστευσαν – *Present – This is an ongoing activity in the present time of the speaker.*

John 4:42 And said unto the woman, Now we believe, not because of thy saying: for we have heard him ourselves, and know that this is indeed the Christ, the <u>Saviour</u> of the world.

- σωτηρ – Not just for the Jews. **See** *Luke 2:11*

The Laver of Brass.

The Laver of the Taabernacle.
John 5:1– 47 The Laver and the Third One Needing A Washing – The Impotent Man.
Jesus' Galilean Ministry. 28– 29 AD.

He explained, "The Son can do nothing by himself; he can do only what he sees his Father doing, because whatever the Father does the Son also does" (John 5:19). "Jesus did the same activities that God the Father did, He helped the helpless, he hopeless and healed the sick, Jesus mirrored the Father, and we are called to mirror. (Ephesians 5:1– 2). As we grow closer to Jesus, we start reflecting on Him. We will develop a deep desire to help others. Our hearts will break for the same things that break His. We will grow more merciful, loving, friendly, and patient. Just as a child learns to mimic their parents, it'll start by changing what we will do. Then, it will en d by changing who we are. Our life should reflect our relationship with Christ. Love like He loves. Forgive as He forgives. Pray as He prayed.

Sacrifice as He sacrificed. Through the Spirit, God has empowered you to live like the Son." *Adapted Edited Source Unknown*

*John 5:1– 47 The Laver – The Third Man with a Crippled Faith – **The** Impotent Man.*
The Healing at the Pool on the Sabbath.

Exodus 30:17– 18 And the LORD spake unto Moses, saying, Thou shalt also makea laver
of brass, and his foot also of brass, to wash withal: and thou shalt put it between the
Tabernacle of the congregation and the altar, and thou shalt put water therein.

– "This laver provided for the priests alone. But in the new dispensation, all believers
are priests, and hence the apostle exhorts them how to draw near to God. See *John
13:10; Heb. 10:22.*"
Jamison, Fauset, and Brown https://www.blueletterbible.org/Comm/jfb/Jhn/Jhn_000.cf
– brass – "Brass was introduced around 500 BC.
– Brass and made from an alloy of Copper and Zinc."
Jamison, Fauset, and Brown https://www.blueletterbible.org/Comm/jfb/Jhn/Jhn_000.cfm
– Some Translations use the word, Bronze. Bronze is a metal alloy consisting primarily
of copper, usually with tin as the main additive. Bronze is an alloy of consisting
primarily of copper, usually with tin as the main additive.
https://interviewmania.com/discussion/53182-chemistry- chemistry-miscellaneous
– The Sumerians called themselves the Sag– giga, the "black-headed ones."
– They were among the first to use Bronze.
– "Around 3500 BC, the first signs of bronze usage by the ancient Sumerians called
"black– headed-ones" appeared in the Tigris Euphrates valley in Western Asia." Edited
from many sites re:"black– headed-ones.
https://guillaumeboivin.com/what-was-bronze-first-used-for.htm.l

John 5:1 After this there was a feast of the Jews, and Jesus went up to Jerusalem. After this
there was a feast of the Jews, and Jesus went up to Jerusalem.

– John uses the Tabernacle with the five pillars past the Entrance Gate of the courtyard.
See Exodus 26:37.
– The Pool of Bethesda, John 5:2. with its five rows of supporting columns of the Pool of
Siloam around the Pool, recently identified, is located just outside of the old city walls.
– The pool "was part of an Asclepion – a healing center dedicated to the Greco–Roman
god of well-being and health. The god's mythical daughters included the goddesses
Hygeia and Panacea. We can hear in their Greek names our modern words for "hygiene"
and "panacea." *Dr. Eli Lizorkin Eyzenberg*
Asclepius's cult of health and healing Judaism and Paganism in Ancient
Jerusalem.

- Theatre of Epidaurus is a theatre in the Greek city of Epidaurus, located on the southeast end of the sanctuary dedicated to the ancient Greek God of medicine, Asclepius.
- Justin Martyr mentions Asclepius saying, "And when he - the devil brings forward the Æsculapius as the raiser of the dead and healer of all diseases, may I do not say that in this matter likewise he has imitated the prophecies about Christ?"

Justin Martyr, Dialogue with Trypho, the Jew, 69.

- Jesus' third sign by the pool of Bethesda is "house of the graceful waters.
- The five porches remind us of the five pillars at the entrance to the Tabernacle proper. *Exodus 26:37 And thou shalt make for the hanging five pillars of shittim wood, and overlay them with gold, and their hooks shall be of gold: and thou shalt cast five sockets of brass for them.*

John 5:1– 15 The Pool of Siloam – The Sabbath Controversy – His healing of a lame man.

- The three other Sabbath healings – *See* Matt. 12:9-13; Mark **3**:1-6; Luke 6:6-11.

John 5:1 After this there was a feast of the Jews; and Jesus went up to Jerusalem.

- All Jewish men required to attend – See Deut. 16:16.
- This is one of the seven feasts of Israel. Jesus' second visit to Jerusalem.
- Jerusalem was yet standing, and not taken and destroyed by the Romans when John wrote his Gospel. Otherwise, it is argued, he would have said, "There was at Jerusalem."
- The Roman Legions of Titus destroyed Jerusalem in 70 AD. They spared only Herod's tower fortress as a symbol of the strength of the Romans who were able to overpower it." Edited *https://bible-history.com/sketches/herods-theater*
- Bethesda – Βηθεσδά – House of Mercy – Healing.

John 5:2 Now there is at Jerusalem by the sheep market a pool, which is called in the Hebrew tongue Bethesda, having five porches.

- is – ἔστι – *Present – This is an ongoing activity in the present time of the speaker.*

John 5:3 In these lay a great multitude of impotent folk, of blind, halt, withered, waiting for the moving of the water.

- lay – κατέκειτο – to lie down
- impotent – ἀσθενούντων – to be feeble
- blind – τυφλῶν – opaque – as if smoky

- halt – χωλῶν – limping
- withered – χωλῶν – dry and wasted

John 5:4 For an <u>angel</u> went down at a certain season into the pool, and troubled the water: whosoever then first after the troubling of the water stepped in was made whole of whatsoever disease he had.

- angel – ἄγγελος – A messenger from God or from the Temple?
- Was this occurrence only on Sabbath days?
- "The pool of Bethesda, "house of mercy" in Hebrew, does not have to be a Jewish site at all, but rather a Greek Asclepion – affiliated facility.
  https://blog.israelbiblicalstudies.com/jewish– studies/Bethesda-pool/beth-shrine-asclepius.
- Was the Bethesda Pool in Jerusalem a shrine of Asclepius?
- "It, therefore, appears that, while the Pool of Bethesda was a pagan place an Asclepion, the Pool of Siloam was indeed connected with the Jerusalem Temple. Of course, Jerusalem was the center for the Ioudaioi *[Judeans]*. in Jesus' days, but it was also, the center for Hellenized ideals in Judea and was under strict Roman control."
  https://israelstudycenter.com/the – pool – of – Bethesda.
- "It is very important to notice that in the healing recorded in chapter of John's Gospel, Jesus does not command the one He healed to wash himself pool of Bethesda, while in the story of the healing of the blind man in chapter nine, he did issue a direct command to go and wash at the pool of Siloam."
  Paganism in Jerusalem .www.beitariel.co.za/articles/paganism-jerusalem-pool-bethesda.
- "It, therefore, appears that while the Pool of Bethesda was a pagan place an Asclepion., the pool of Siloam was indeed connected with the Jerusalem Temple – sabbath-healing-at-the-Bethesda-pool." *greekmedicine.net.*
- "The stirring up of the water was part of a ceremony when the priests of the Asclepiu temple opened the connecting pipes between the higher and the lower portions of the pool. Because one set of pipes was higher than the other, this caused a "stirring" of the water in the pool' *greekmedicine.net.*
- "The water in the upper reservoir would flow into the lower portion of the pool.
- A 5th century Christian scribe would not know that." *greekmedicine.net.*

John 5:5– 18 The Sign of Authority.
John 5:5 And a certain man was there, which had an <u>infirmity</u> thirty and eight years.

- infirmity – ἀσθενεία – feebleness – without strength

John 5:6 When Jesus saw him lie, and knew that he had been now a long time in that case, he saith unto him, Wilt thou be made whole?

- "Dost thou wish to become whole?" *Robertson's Word Pictures—StudyLight.org.*
- Wilt – Θελεις – desire – Does he desire to be whole? Why are you here?
- Have you made any effort to be on the edge of the pool?
- Did they feel that God was the cause of his impotence?
- "God is most often identified source for disease and healing [Exodus 15:26], The most common cause for God sending disease is sin Deut. 32:39. God flatly declares, "I wound and I heal."
  Jewish Healing & Magic www.myjewishlearning.com/article/jewish-healing-magic.

The Man with a crippled faith, and no one willing to help him.
John 5:7 The <u>impotent</u> man answered him, Sir, I have no man, when the water is troubled, to <u>put</u> me into the pool: but while I am coming, another steppeth down before me.

- impotent – ασθενεω – without strength – feeble
- put me – βάλη – "that he throws me in." *Robertson's Word Pictures StudyLight.org.*

John 5:8 Jesus saith unto him, <u>Rise take up</u> thy bed, and <u>walk</u>. – Rise – ἔγειρε – Aorist Mid. Imperative – This is a punctiliar point-in-

- take up – lift up – ἆρον – *Aorist Mid. – Imperative – This is a punctiliar point-in-time activity, a command.*
- walk – περιπάτει – *Present Imperative – This is an ongoing activity in the present time of the speaker, a command.*

John 5:9 And immediately the man was made whole, and took up his bed, and walked: and on the same day was the sabbath. "The first of the violations of the Sabbath rules of the Jews by Jesus in Jerusalem."
  www.meaningfullife.com/chapter-one-text-ethics-of-our-fathers/
  Talmud Mishnah Sabbath c. 10. sect. 3..

- These laws of the Sanhedrin occur during the Fifth Century BC.
- Halakha – Jewish law. identifies thirty– nine categories of activity prohibited on the Shabbat. *www.ou.org/holidays/the_thirty_nine_categories_of_sabbath_work_prohibited*

The opposition of the Jews.
John 5:10 The Jews therefore said unto him that was <u>cured</u>, It is the sabbath day: it is not <u>lawful</u> for thee to carry thy bed.

- cured – τεθεραπευμένῳ – *Perfect Tense – A completed action with continuing effects.*
- lawful – ἔξεστί – According to the Pharisees.

John 5:11– 13 The testimony of the man-made whole.
John 5:11 He answered them, He that made me whole, the same said unto me, Take up thy bed, and <u>walk</u>.

- walk – περιπάτε – walking around.

John 5:12 Then asked they him, What man is that which said unto thee, <u>Take</u> up thy bed, and <u>walk</u>?

- take – αρον – *Aorist – This is a punctiliar point-in-time activity.*
- walk – περιπατει – *Present Imperative – This is an ongoing activity, a command.*

John 5:13 And he that <u>was healed</u> wist not who it was: for Jesus had conveyed himself away, a multitude g being in that place. – healed – ἰαθεὶς – Aorist Pass. Part. – This is a punctiliar point-in-time activity.

John 5:14 Afterward, Jesus findeth him in the <u>temple</u> and said unto him, Behold, thou art made whole <u>sin</u> no more, lest a worse thing come unto thee.

- temple – ἱερόν – The sacred place.
- sin – ἁμαρτάνω – A sin general. The definite article is missing.
- Jesus says his weakness was the result of sin. What sin?
- The effect of the washing in the Laver. We are washed in the Word is to be cleansed.
- *Psalm 19:9. "How shall a young man cleanse his way? By taking heed according to Your word."*

John 5:15 The man <u>departed</u>, and told the Jews that it was Jesus, which had made him <u>whole</u>. – departed – ἀπῆλθεν – Aorist – This is a punctiliar point-in-time activity.

- whole – ὑγιῆ – healthy

John 5:16 And therefore did the Jews [Judeans] *persecute Jesus, and sought to slay him, because he had done these things on the <u>sabbath</u> day.*

- Every Sabbath day?
- persecute – ἐδίωκον – began to persecute.
- slay – αποκτειναι – Aorist – *This is a punctiliar point-in-time activity.*
- "Any procedure which is necessary to perform for the patient, but it is clear that it does not at all need to be performed on Shabbat, … "should be delayed until after Shabbat. If a person is ill before Shabbat and he will need care on Shabbat that will include acts forbidden on Shabbat."

The 39 Acts Forbidden on the Sabbath.
https://theisraelbible.com › the-39-acts-forbidden-on-the Sabbath.

- *"The Testimony of the Father to the Son – The work of God is to restore."*

Jewish Savings Lives–on–Shabbabot.

John 5:17 But Jesus answered them, My Father <u>worketh</u> hitherto, and I <u>work</u>. – worketh – ἐργάζεται – *Aorist – This is a punctiliar point-in-time activity.*

- work – ἐργάζομαι – is working – *Present – This is an ongoing activity in the present time of the speaker.*
- The testimony of the Jews. [Judeans]

Jesus Is Equal with God.
John 5:18 Therefore, the Jews <u>sought</u> the more to kill him, because he not only had <u>broken</u> the sabbath, but said also that God was his Father, making himself equal with God.

- Sought the more – ἐζήτουν – and continued to seek
- broken – ἔλυε – to loosen – *Imperfect – A past action or state which is incomplete.*

John 5:19– 34 Does not directly deal with the Tabernacle.
John 5:35 He was a burning and a shining light: and ye were <u>willing</u> for a season to rejoice in his light.

- willing – ηθελησατε – *Aorist – This is a punctiliar point-in-time activity.*
- "But ye became willing."
- season – ὥραν – hour

The Table of Shewbread.
John 6:1– 72 Table of Shewbread– Spring 29 AD. Jesus Feeds the Five Thousand.
John 6:1 After these things Jesus went over <u>the sea</u> <u>of Galilee</u>, which is the sea of Tiberias. Sea of Galilee – Gennesaret in Luke 5:1 and "Sea of Tiberias" as in John 1:1.

John 6:2 And a great multitude <u>followed</u> him, because they saw his miracles which he did on them that were diseased.

- followed – the crowd. – ηκολουθει – *Imperfect – A past action or state which is incomplete.*

John 6:3 And Jesus went up into a mountain, and there he <u>sat</u> with his disciples.

- sat – εκαθητο – *Imperfect – A past action which is incomplete.* "He was sitting."

John 6:4 And the <u>passover</u>, a feast of the Jews, was nigh.

- Jesus' third Passover.

John 6:5 When Jesus then <u>lifted</u> <u>up</u> his eyes, and saw a great company <u>come</u> unto him, he saith unto Philip, Whence shall we buy <u>bread,</u> that these may eat?

- lifted up – ἐπάρας – *Aorist Part. – This is a punctiliar point-in-time activity.*
- He looked down from the mountain.
- is coming – ερχεται – *Present – This is an ongoing activity in the present time of the speaker.*
- Bethsaida is about six miles away.
- bread – ἔρχεται – plural – loaves of bread.
- "They that follow Christ do sometime hunger, but they are never destitute of help."
  Geneva Study Bible John 6:5 [notes].

John 6:6 And this he said to <u>prove</u> him: for he himself knew what he would do.

- prove – πειραζων – testing – proving – *Present Participle, An action that is currently taking place, indicating a habit.*
- "Christ often tests us to see what we shall say and do in the presence of overwhelming difficult . . ." *F. B. Meyer biblehub.com/commentaries/ttb/john/18.htm.*

John 6:7 Philip answered him, <u>Two hundred pennyworth</u> of bread is not sufficient for them, that every one of them may take a little.

- Two hundred pennyworth – δηναριων – A day's labor.

John 6:8 One of his disciples, Andrew, Simon Peter's brother, saith unto him,

- The Gospels of Matt., Mark, and Luke say this answer is to all the apostles.
- Both are from Bethsaida, along with Philip.

John 6:9 There is a <u>lad</u> here, which hath five <u>barley</u> loaves, and two <u>small fishes</u>: but what are they among so many?

- lad – παιδαριον – The Iota "ι,i" means they are small fishes.
- barley – κριθίνους – A cereal grain.
- Was he employed to carry the disciple's provisions?
- Why is he a part of the group of followers?
- small – fishes – οψαρια – Only in John.
- fishes – οψαρ<u>ι</u>α – small – The iota "ι,i" makes it a small boat.

John 6:10 And Jesus said, Make the men <u>sit down</u>. Now there was much grass in the place. So the men sat down, in number about five thousand.

- sit down – αναπεσειν – recline – [2]*Aorist Infinitive – This is a punctiliar point-in-time activity.*

John 6:11 And Jesus took the loaves; and when he had <u>given thanks,</u> he distributed to the disciples, and the disciples to them that were set down; and likewise of the fishes as much as they would.

- given thanks – εὐχαριστήσας
- Deut. 8:10 – The usual grace said before meals.

*https://www.jewishencyclopedia.com/articles/6843-**grace**-at-meal*

- "The Jews had a custom of leaving something for those that served."

Robertson's Word Pictures—StudyLight.org

John 6:12 When they were filled, he said unto his disciples, Gather up the <u>fragments</u> that remain, that nothing be lost.

- the fragments that remained – More provided than needed.
- "The Jews had a custom of leaving something for those that served."
  Robertson's Word Pictures www.studylight.org/commentaries/eng/rwp/john.html.

John 6:13 Therefore they gathered them together, and filled twelve baskets with the fragments of the five barley loaves, which remained over and above unto them that had eaten.

- twelve baskets – One or each disciple.
- Food for the Twelve – More food at the end than at the beginning.

Bethsaida Wilderness to the Plain of Gennesaret.
John 6:14 Then those men, when they had seen the miracle that Jesus did, said, This is of a truth that prophet that <u>should</u> <u>come</u> into the world.

- should come – ερχομενος – *Present Part. – An action that is currently taking place.*
- The one that is coming.

John 6:15–21 Jesus Walks on Water. From the Gennesaret Plain to Capernaum.
John 6:22– 35 I Am the Bread of Life.

- The Place: Jesus goes to the mountain. verse 15.
- The purpose is to pray, – προσ + εύχομαι – To pray towards God.
- The conditions of the sea. – verses 16 – 18.
- The control of Jesus over the sea. – verses 19 – 21.

John 6:22 The day following, when the people which stood on the other side of the sea saw that there was none other <u>boat</u> there, save that one where into his disciples were entered, and that Jesus went not with his disciples into the boat, but that his disciples were gone away alone;

- boat – πλοιάριον – The use of iota "ι,i" makes it a "little" boat.

John 6:23 Howbeit there came other boats from Tiberias nigh unto the place where they did eat bread, after that the Lord had <u>given</u> <u>thanks</u>:

- had given thanks – εὐχαριστήσαντος – *Aorist Participle – This is a punctiliar point-in-time activity.*

John 6:24 When the people therefore saw <u>that</u> Jesus was not there, neither his disciples, they also took shipping, and came to Capernaum, <u>seeking</u> for Jesus. – that – ὅτι – because that

- seeking – ζητοῦντες – *Present Participle – An action that is currently taking place, and indicating a habit.*

John 6:25 And when they <u>had found</u> him on the other side of the sea, they said unto him, Rabbi when <u>camest</u> thou hither?

- had found – εὑρόντες – *Aorist Participle – This is a punctiliar point-in-time activity.*
- camest – γέγονας – *Perfect Tense – A completed action with continuing effects.*
- When hast thou come?
- We sought you anxiously on the other side of the lake and could not see how you came across.

John 6:30 They said therefore unto him, What sign shewest thou then, <u>that</u> we <u>may see</u>, and <u>believe</u> thee? what dost thou work?

- that – ἵνα – in-order-that
- may see – ἴδωμεν – *Aorist Subjunctive – This is a potential punctiliar point-in-time activity.*
- may believe – πιστεύσωμέν – *Aorist Subj. – This is a potential punctiliar point-in-time activity.*

John 6:31 Our fathers did eat <u>manna</u> in the desert; as it is <u>written</u>, He gave them bread from heaven to eat.

- "pot on manna" This word is on the lentil of an old Syrian synagogue.
- Manna was preserved in the Ark of the Covenant. – See Exodus 16:32.
- written – γεγραμμέν – *Perfect Participle – A completed action with continuing effects.*
- ον – *Perfect Participle – A completed action with continuing effects.*

John 6:32 Then Jesus said unto them, Verily, verily, I say unto you, Moses <u>gave</u> you not that bread from heaven; but my Father giveth you the true bread from heaven.

- gave – δίδωσιν – *Perfect Tense – A completed action with continuing effects.*

John 6:33 For the <u>bread</u> of God is he which cometh down from heaven, and giveth the unto the world.

- bread – ἄρτος – the bread – ὁ ἄρτος – The word s masculine.

John 6:34 Then said they unto him, Lord, evermore <u>give</u> us this bread.

- give – δίδωσιν – ²*Aorist Imperative – A punctiliar point-in-time activity* with *command.*

John 6:35 And Jesus said unto them, <u>I am</u> the bread of life: he that cometh to me shall never hunger; and he that believeth on me shall never thirst.

- I am – εἰμι – *Present -- This is an ongoing activity in the present time of the speaker.*

John 7:1– 53 Jesus at the Feast of Booths [Tabernacles]. Six Months after 6:
Jesus' Declaration concerning himself during the Feast of Sukkot – Tabernacles.

The Feast of Sukkot is celebrated on the 15th day of the seventh month.
   Tishrei – Sept. 14 - Oct. 15. The days of rest Shabbat or Sabbath.
The people of Israel dwell in temporary shelters. Remembering the wilderness journey from Egypt to the Promise Land.
Lev. 23:43 That your generations may know that I made the children of Israel to dwell in booths, when I brought them out of the land of Egypt: I am the LORD your God.

John 7:1-10 Before the Feast; 7:11-39; During the Feast; 7:40-53. After the Feast.;
John 7:1 After these things Jesus walked in Galilee: for he would not walk in Jewry, because the Jews sought to kill him.

- Recorded in – See 5:18.
- Jewry – The Jewish population in Judea.

Rodney F. Price, D.Min.

John 7:2 Now the Jews' feast of <u>tabernacles</u> was at hand.
    The **Feast** of Sukkot is celebrated on the 15th day of the seventh month of Tishrei.

- A week-long celebration.

John 7:3 His brethren therefore said unto him, <u>Depart</u> hence, and go into Judaea, that thy Disciples also may <u>see</u> the works that thou doest.

- Depart – remove – *Aorist Imperative* – *a* command.
- see – θεωρέω – As spectators – *Aorist Subjunctive* – *Expresses punctiliar situations that are hypothetical or not yet realized.*

***John 7:4** For there is <u>no</u> man that doeth anything in secret, and he himself <u>seeketh</u> to <u>be known openly</u>. If thou do these things, shew thyself to the world.*

- No – οὐδείς – **Not even one**
- seeketh – ζητέω – *Present* – *An ongoing activity.*
- **be** known openly – ἐν παῤῥησίᾳ – *bluntness, publicitly.*

John 7:5 For <u>neither</u> did his brethren <u>believe</u> in him.

- neither – οὐδέ – not even – believe – επιστευον – *Imperfect* – *A past action which is incomplete* [were believing]
- James, Joses (a form of Joseph), Simon, and Jude, and unnamed sisters. Matt. 13:56.

John 7:6 Then Jesus said unto them, My <u>time</u> is not yet come: but your time is <u>alway</u> <u>ready.</u>

- time – καιρὸς – *A set or proper time.*
- alway ready – at hand – ετοιμος
- "A regular Jewish obligation to go up to the feast."
      Robertson's Word Pictures www.studylight.org/commentaries/eng/rwp/john.html.
    "With Me it is otherwise; on every movement of Mine there hangs what ye know not. The world has no quarrel with you, for ye bear no testimony against it, and so draw down upon yourselves none of its wrath; but I am here to lift up My voice against its hypocrisy, and denounce its abominations; therefore it cannot endure Me, and one false step might precipitate its fury on its Victim's head before the time. Away, therefore, to the feast as soon as it suits you; I follow at the fitting moment, but 'My time is not yet full come."
    Jamieson, Fauset, and Brown. www.blueletterbible.org/Comm/jfb/Jhn/Jhn_000.cfm.

John 7:7 The world cannot <u>hate</u> you; but me it <u>hateth,</u> because I testify of it, that the works thereof are evil.

- hate – hateth – to persecute – *Present Act. Infinitive.*
- John 15:18.

John 7:8 Go ye up <u>unto</u> this feast: I go not up yet unto this feast; for my time is not yet full come.

- unto – *eis* – into
- "not yet been fulfilled" *Dr. Bullinger in ww.studylight.org/commentaries/eng/bul/ john-7.*

John 7:9 When he had said these words unto them, he <u>abode</u> still in Galilee.

- abode – εμεινεν – In a given place – *Aorist Mid. – This is a punctiliar point-in-time activity and covers a period of some days.*

John 7:10 But when his brethren <u>were gone up</u>, then went he also up unto the feast, not openly, but as it were in secret.

- were gone up – ανεβησαν – *Aorist Mid. – This is a punctiliar point-in-time activity.*
- up – ανεβη – *Aorist Mid. – This is a punctiliar point-in-time activity. John 7:11 Then the Jews <u>sought</u> him at the feast, and said, Where is he?*
- sought – εζητουν – *Imperfect – Action in the past which is incomplete.*

John 7:12-13 Is omitted.
John 7:14 Now about the midst of the feast Jesus went up into the temple, and <u>taught</u>. – taught – εδιδασκεν – Imperfect – Action in the past which is incomplete.
John 7:15-36 Is omitted John 7:37 In the last day, that great day of the feast, Jesus <u>stood</u> and <u>cried</u>, saying, any man thirst, <u>let</u> him <u>come</u> unto me, and <u>drink.</u>

- stood – ἵστημι – *Imperfect – Action in the past which is incomplete.*
- cried – εκραξε – *Aorist – A point-in-time activity.*
- let come – ἔρχομαι – *Imperfect – Action in the past which is incomplet.*
- drink – πινετω – *Present Mid. Imperative – A command in a point-in-time.*

John 7:38 He that believeth on me, as the scripture hath said, out of his belly <u>shall flow</u> rivers of living water.

- *shall flow – ῥεύσουσιν – Present Act. Subj. – Expresses punctiliar situations that are hypothetical or not yet realized.*

John 7:39 - 51. Is omitted.

John 7:52 They <u>answered</u> and <u>said</u> unto him, Art thou also of Galilee? <u>Search,</u> and <u>look</u>: for out of Galilee <u>ariseth</u> no prophet.

- *answered – ἀπεκρίθησαν – Aorist Middle – A point-in-time activity.*
- *said – εἶπον – [2]Aorist – A point-in-time activity.*
- *look – εἶ – Present Subjunctive – Expresses punctiliar situations that are hypothetical or not yet realized.*
- seek – *ἐραύνησον – Aorist Mid. – A point-in-time activity.* – *ἴδε – Aorist Mid. – A point-in-time activity.*
- see *ariseth – ἐγήγερται – Perf. Pass.* – "but this is false, for Jonah the prophet **of the** Grathhepher which was in the tribe of Zebulun, which tribe was in Galilee;
- **See** 2Kings 14:25.

     And the Jews (z) themselves say that Jonah, the son of Amittai, was, מזבולון, of "Zebulun", and that his father was of Zebulun, and his mother was of Asher (a); both which tribes were in Galilee: and if no prophet had, as yet, arose from thence, it did not follow that no one should arise: besides, there is a prophecy in which it was foretold, that a prophet, and even the Messiah, the great light, should arise in Galilee; see Isa. 9:1; and they themselves say, that the Messiah should be revealed in Galilee;"

     John Gill (z) T. Hieros. Succa, fol. 55. 1, (a) Bereshit Rabba, sect. 98. fol. 85. 4.

The Golden Candlestick.

Jesus is The Light of the World.
John 8:1

NOTE – The Textus Receptus includes this passage as in the majority of the Greek texts.
*The passage is omitted in most Minority Texts.

"The religious leaders, try to trap Jesus as they publicly shame a woman caught in adultery. The religious leaders are exercising spiritual abuse, first by shaming the woman and then by trying to undermine the credibility of Jesus. Jesus, recognizing their horrific abuse of spiritual power, avoids their trap by ignoring them at first. "Let any one of who is without sin be the first to throw a stone."

He is saying, "Your power abuse prevents you from receiving God's grace. Confess your sin, surrender that godless power, and you can find life."

Edited Unknown Source

"The meek, life– transforming Savior invites everyone to die and truly live! Who could have known that meekness could be so radically renewing?

https://todaydevotional.com

John 8:1 – 11 The woman was taken in adultery and forgiven of adultery. The setting is the Temple during the Feast of the Tabernacles.

"The religious leaders, try to trap Jesus as they publicly shame a woman caught in adultery. The religious leaders are exercising spiritual abuse, first by shaming the woman and then by trying to undermine the credibility of Jesus. Jesus, recognizing their horrific abuse of spiritual power, avoids their trap by ignoring them at first. "Let anyone of who is without sin be the first to throw a stone." He is saying, "Your power abuse prevents you from receiving God's grace. Confess your sin, surrender that godless power, and you can find life."

Edited Unknown Source

"The meek, life–transforming Savior invites everyone to die and truly live! Who could have known that meekness could be so radically renewed."

https.todaydevotional.com

John 8:1 Jesus goes to the Mount of Olives.

- Was Jesus lodging at the house of Mary, Martha, and Lazarus?

John 8:1 Jesus goes to the Mount of Olives.

- Jesus will replace the Candlestick of the Tabernacle.
  Rev. 21:23 And the city had no need of the sun, neither of the moon, to shine in it: for the <u>glory</u> of God did lighten it, and the Lamb is the <u>light</u> <u>thereof</u>.
- *glory – Shekinah?*
- light – λυχνος – *A lamp.*
- In the Court of the Women stood two immense menorot(ah) – lampstands.
- ".. while these majestic lampstands were still lit, to point to his own messianic purpose to be "the light of the world.""
- The Roman historian Tacitus – 110 AD – declared that the temple "possessed enormous riches. *cojs.org/110-c-e-tacitus-56-c-e-120-c-e14_commentary*
- The water is drawn and poured over the altar in a special ceremony

John 8:2 And early in the morning the next day he came again into the temple grounds. and all the people came unto him; and he <u>sat</u> <u>down</u>, and taught them.

- temple – ἱερόν – *Temple grounds.*
- sat down – καθίσας taught – *Aorist Part. – A point-in-time activity.*

- "After the eighth and last day of the feast." *Robertson's Word Pictures StudyLight.org* – taught – ἐδίδασκεν – *Imperfect – Action in the past which is incomplete.*
- ***Jesus*** continued to teach.

John 8:3 And the scribes and" the Pharisees brought unto him a <u>woman</u> <u>taken</u> in adultery; and when they had <u>set</u> her in the midst,

- woman – γυνή – *She is a married woman.*
- taken – κατειλημμένην – taken – *Perf. Pass. – completed action with continuing results.*
- "Two persons at least, who could be witnesses of it; otherwise, the accusation was not legal; see Deut.17:" *Gill's Exposition 8:4 (biblehub.com)*
- The two men who caught the couple were not mentioned.

John 8:4 They say unto him, Master, this woman was <u>taken</u> <u>the</u> <u>very</u> <u>act</u>.

- *Process of the Law – Numb. 5:1.*
- was taken – κατελήφθη – caught and still guilty – *Perf. Pass. – Completed action.*
- very act – αὐτοφώρῳ – She was caught in the very act of adultery.
- Was this a setup to catch her?

John 8:5 Now Moses in the law Deut. 2:23. commanded us, that such should be stoned: but what sayest thou?

- *Lev 20:10 And the man that committeth adultery with another man's wife, even he that committeth adultery with his neighbour's wife, the adulterer and the adulteress shall surely be put to death.*
- "Simply put to death, but in aggravated cases, at least in later times, this was probably by stoning." See *Ezek. 16:40.*
- Yet only by Roman Law in Jesus' day.
  Jamenson, Fausset, and Brown www.blueletterbible.org/Comm/jfb/Jhn/Jhn_000.cfm
- They were using this question as a trap.

John 8:6 This they said, tempting him, that they might have to accuse him. But Jesus stooped down, and with his finger wrote on the <u>ground</u> paved stones., as though he heared them not.

- ground – γην – The paved stones of the Temple.
  www.bible.ca/archeology/bible-archeology

John 8:7 So when they continued asking him, he lifted up himself and said unto them, He that is without sin among you, let him first cast a stone at her.

- lifted up himself – ἀνέκυψεν – *Aorist Act. Part. – A point-in-time activity.*
- *Jesus was seated – John 8:2. – – Note –* Without a definite article, therefore, it is sin in general.
- him – Jesus then picks out the executioner in the case.

John 8:8 And again he stooped down and wrote on the ground. – wrote – ἔγραφεν – *"Imperf. of katagraphō,* an *old compound, here only in N.T, to draw, to delineate, to write down." Robertson's Word Pictures—StudyLight.org*

- "Jer. 17:13, *"O LORD, the hope of Israel, all that forsake thee shall be ashamed,* **and** *they that depart from me shall be written in the earth, because they have forsaken the LORD, the fountain of living waters. –* "It could be that Christ was writing their names in the earth, thus fulfilling this prophecy in Jeremiah. They knew the Old Testament and this passage and were convicted in their hearts." *John Gill https://www. biblestudytools.com/john*

John 8:9 And they which heard it, being convicted by their own conscience, went out one by one, beginning at the eldest, even unto the last: and Jesus was left alone, and the woman standing in the midst. of scribes and Pharisees.

- went out – ἐξήρχοντο – *Imperfect – A past action or state which is incomplete.*
- woman – γυνή – *A married woman.*

John 8:10 When Jesus had lifted up himself, and saw none but the woman he said unto her, Woman where are those thine accusers? hath no man condemned thee? – woman – γυνή – *A married woman.*

- condemned – κατέκρινεν – *Aorist – A point-in-time activity.*

John 8:11 She said, No man, Lord. And Jesus said unto her, Neither do I condemn thee: go, and sin, no more.

- sin – ἁμάρτανε – *Present Tense – ongoing activity.*
- *Without a definite article, therefore, sin in general.*

- "He has to choose either to allow the woman to go free and publicly disobey the law or to approve of her killing and forfeit his reputation as a friend to sinners and possibly risking trouble with Rome for contributing to a capital punishment that they had not sanctioned." *https://www.bibleodyssey.org/en/passages/related*
- Lord – Κύριε – A polite way to address any man.
  Num. 5:13 And a man lie with her carnally, and it be hid from the eyes
- Not referring to Christ as God.
- Since there were not two accusers – Jesus did not judge her – but he warned her.
- *See also John 5:13,14; 5:22*
- *Numbers 5:13 And a man lie with her carnally, and it be hid from the eyes of her husband, and be kept close, and she be defiled, and **there be** no witness against her, neither she be taken with the manner;of her husband, and be kept close, and she be defiled, and <u>there be no witness against</u> her, neither she be taken with the manner; John 8:12 Then spake Jesus again unto them, saying, I am the light of the world: he that followeth me shall not walk in darkness. but shall have the light of life.*
  John 1:4 In him was life; and the <u>life</u> was the light of men.
- life – ζωὴ – This is life in the absolute sense.

John the Baptist's comments about Christ being the Light.

- The "I am" statements – εγω ειμι – *Present – This is an ongoing activity in the present time of the speaker.*

John 6:35 – I am the bread of life.

John 8:12 – I am the light of the world.

John 10:7,9 – I am the door.

John 10:11,14 – I am the good shepherd.

John 11:25 – I am the resurrection.

John 13:19 – I am he.

John 9:1– 41 The Golden Candlestick.
>   Jesus does something that only God can do. Jesus Heals a Man Born Blind.
>   The Golden Candlestick – Jesus is the Light of World for those following Him.
>   John the Baptist's comments about Christ being the Light.

John 1:4 In him was <u>life</u>; and the life was the light of men.

-   life – ζωὴ – This is life in the absolute sense.

John 1:5 And the light shineth in darkness; and the darkness comprehended it not.

-   shineth – φαίνει – shining – *Present – This is an ongoing activity in the present time of the speaker.*
-   Previous References that Jesus is the Light. Jn. 1:4,1:5,7,8,9, 3:19,20,21, 5:35.

John 9:1 And as Jesus <u>passed</u> by, he saw a man which was blind <u>from</u> his birth.

-   passed by – παράγων – *Present – This is an ongoing activity in the present time of the speaker.*
-   from – ἐκ – out of

John 9:2 And his disciples asked him, saying, Master, who did sin, this man, or his parents, that he was <u>born</u> blind?

-   "This is the only example of congenital blindness healed." R*obertson's Word Pictures StudyLight.org*
-   "it is sometimes true that disease is the result of personal sin as in the man." *Robertson's Word Pictures*
-   Job's friends believed this was the cause of his problems.
-   "Jewish view that the merits or demerits of the parents would appear in the children, and that the thoughts of a mother might affect the moral state of her unborn offspring." *Olam Ha Ba; The After Life jfaq.org,*

John 9:3 Jesus answered, Neither hath this man <u>sinned</u>, nor his <u>parents</u>: <u>but</u> that the works of God should be made manifest in him.

- born in sins – <u>ἐν ἁμαρτίαις</u> – The word is plural.
- Therefore, born of parents not married.
- But – ἀλλ' – But he was born blind.

John 9:4 I must work the works of him that sent me, while it is day: the <u>night</u> <u>cometh</u>, when no man can work.

- night cometh – ἔρχεται νὺξ – The night is coming on – *Present – This is an ongoing activity in the present time of the speaker.*

John 9:5 As <u>long</u> as I am in the world, I am <u>the</u> light of the world.

- long – ὅταν – whenever
  Vincent's Word Studies www.studylight.org/commentaries/eng/vnt/john.html.
- the – The definite article is absent.

John 9:6 When he had thus spoken, he spat on the ground, and made clay of the spittle, and he anointed the eyes of the blind man with the clay,

- He violated the law – Jesus worked on the Sabbath.
- "We have already seen part of the list of thirty– nine forbidden labors of Shabbat."
  https://www.sefaria.org/Mishnah_Shabbat.7.2
  www.meaningfullife.com/chapter-one-text-ethics-of-our-fathers/ Talmud

John 9:7 And said unto him, Go, wash in the pool of <u>Siloam</u>, which is by interpretation, Sent. He went his way, therefore, and <u>washed</u>, and came seeing.

- Siloam – Σιλωάμ – Is located in East Jerusalem.
- "apparently bathing and not merely washing his eyes."
  Robertson's Word Picture www.studylight.org/commentaries/eng/rwp/john.
- washed – νίψαι – "Especially the face and hands."
  Vincent's Word Studies https://www.studylight.org/commentaries/eng/vnt/john.html.

John 9:8–12 The blind man's testimony.

Rodney F. Price, D.Min.

John 9:8 The neighbours therefore, and they which before <u>had seen</u> him that he was blind, said, Is not this he that sat and <u>begged</u>?

- seen – θεωροῦντες – seeing – *Present Participle – This is an ongoing activity in the present time of the speaker indicating a habit.*
- begged – προσαιτῶν – begging – *Present Participle – An action that is crrently taking place indicating a habit.*

John 9:9 Some said, This is he: others said, He is <u>like</u> him: but he said, I am he.

- like – ὅμοιος – Similar in appearance or character.

John 9:10 Therefore said they unto him, How were thine eyes opened?

- "These neighbours admit the fact and want the manner "how" of the cure made clear." *Robertson's Word Picture www.studylight.org/commentaries/eng/rwp/john*
- opened – ἀνεῴχθησάν – *Aorist Passive Ind. – A point-in-time activity.*

John 9:11 He answered and said, A man that is called Jesus made clay, and anointed mine eyes, and said unto me, Go to the pool of Siloam, and wash: and I went and washed, and I received <u>sight</u>.

- sight – ἀνέβλεψα – to lookup – *Aorist A point-in-time activity.*
- "He got back sight that he had never had."
  Robertson's Word Pictures www.studylight.org/commentaries/eng/rwp/john-9.html,

John 9:12 Then said they unto him, Where is he? He said, I <u>know</u> not.

- know – οἶδα – Information
- See John 7:11

The Pharisees Offended and Questioned him and the man's parents.
John 9:13–38 The healing is challenged by the Pharisees.
John 9:13 <u>They</u> brought to the <u>Pharisees</u> him that aforetime was blind.

- They – The neighbors.
- The Seven Types of Pharisees. *Babylonian Talmud, Sota 22b*

  https://halakhah.com/sotah/sotah_22.html

1. He was criticized for hypocrisy.
   The Showy Pharisee. They were worried about the outward show of their faith.
2. Criticized for false humility.
   The Stumbling Pharisees. They walk around always hanging their heads down & thus often fell and show their injuries and brokenness as sacrifices for God.
3. He is criticized for false piety.
   The Bleeding Nose Pharisees. They were so afraid they might lust that they would turn their heads when they saw a pretty girl and would run into something.
4. He is criticized for false separation. The Mortar and Pestle Pharisees wore a cap covering their eyes to avoid seeing sinful activities.
5. He is criticized for pride.
   The Pharisees of fear were so in awe of God that they strove obedience.
6. He is criticized for self-rightness.
   They had such a deep relationship with God that their righteous behavior was a natural response to their love for Him.
7. He is criticized for unfounded fear. They kept the law because of fear of future judgment.

Edited from www.christiantoday.com/article/7-familiar-types-of-pharisee

John 9:14– 17 The prejudice of the Pharisees, they only saw a Sabbath violation.
John 9:14 And it was <u>the</u> sabbath day when Jesus made the clay, and opened his eyes.

- the – sabbath day is without a definite article.
- opened – ἀνέῳξεν – *Aorist Mid. – A point-in-time activity.*

John 9:15 Then again, the Pharisees also <u>asked</u> him how he had received his sight. He said unto them, He put clay upon mine eyes, and I washed, and do see.

- asked – ἠρώτων – asking – *Present Act. Imperative – A point-in-time activity, a command.*
- "began also to question him."
  Robertson's Word Pictures https://www.studylight.org/commentaries/eng/rwp/john-9.html,

John 9:16 Therefore said some of the Pharisees, This man is not of God, because he keepeth not the Sabbath day. Others said, How can a man that is a sinner do such miracles? And there was a division among them.

- of – εκ – To be from beside.
- others – ἄλλοι – Of the same kind.

John 9:17 They say unto the blind man again, What sayest thou of him, that he hath opened thine eyes? He said, He is <u>a prophet</u>. – a prophet – προφήτης – He is not THE promised Prophet.

John 9:18 – 25 The Parents' Excommunication.

John 9:18 But the Jews [Judeans] *did not believe concerning him, that he had been blind, and received his sight, until they called the parents of him that had received his sight.* – him – "not Jesus – But the blind man."

> *Robertson's Word Pictures www.studylight.org/commentaries/eng/rwp/john-9.html.*

John 9:19 And they asked them, saying, Is this your son, who ye say was born blind? how then doth he now see?

- They asked Jesus three questions.

John 9:20 His parents answered them and said, We <u>know</u> that this is our son, and that he was born blind:

- know – οἴδαμεν – Information –*Perfect – A completed action with continuing effects.*

John 9:21 But by what means he now seeth, we know not; or who hath opened his eyes, we <u>know</u> not: he is of age; ask him: he shall speak for himself.

- know – οἴδαμεν – and continue to know. *Perfect Tense – A completed action with continuing effects at a point in time.*
- "he is of age; at man's estate, as, with the Jews, one was, who was at the age of thirteen years, if he could produce the signs of puberty: and such an one was allowed a witness in any case, but not under this age; nor if he was arrived to it, if the above signs could not be produced. This man very likely was much older, as may be thought from the whole of his conduct, his pertinent answers, and just reasoning, wherefore his parents direct the Sanhedrin to him for an answer to their third question." *John Gill https://biblehub.com/commentaries/john/9-21.htm,*

John 9:22 These words spake his parents, because they feared the Jews [Judeans]*: for the Jews* [Judeans] *had agreed already, that if any man did confess that he was Christ, he should be <u>put out of the synagogue</u>.*

- from the synagogue – ἀποσυνάγωγος – He is kept away from the Synagogue.
- Three types of excommunication.

1. The lightest level was the *neziphah* or *n'zifah* (rebuke) in which a person was removed from seven to thirty days. An individual such as the synagogue president could impose this penalty. A New Testament example is found in 1 Timothy 5:1.

2. A moderate level of punishment was the *niddui* or *niddul* (casting out; rejection) of the congregation. This action is the decision of three Persons, and the excommunication lasted required for an additional thirty days.
    --- A New Testament example as found in Titus 3:10.

3. The most severe form of excommunication was the *"cherem"* which resulted in the excommunicated person being treated as if dead.
    --- A New Testament example found in Matthew 18:15-20
    www.mysteriesofthemessiah.net/2015/12/11—02-23 pharisees-*question-the-healed-mans-parents.*

—   "Talmudic writings speak of two, or rather, we should say, of three, kinds of 'excommunication,' of which the two first were chiefly disciplinary, while the third was the real 'casting out,' 'un-Synagogueing' 'cutting off from the congregation." *Jerusalem Talmud the Moed K. 8.*

https://www.jewishvirtuallibrary.org/talmud-jerusalem.

—   "Excommunication was commonly referred to in the Torah as "herem" The biblical form of excommunicating indicates any person or thing removed.
—   "But punitive measures for miss behaving Jews on Earth?
—   The Talmud offers three forms of Jewish– flavored excommunication for your liking: "nezifah," niddui," and the dreaded "herem"
—   "Though it's up to a rabbinic court to dole out censures, the Talmud helpfully lists a number of transgressions that might elicit one: insulting a learned man; calling a fellow Jew a 'slave'; keeping an object or animal that could harm others, like a broken ladder or a rabid dog; taking God's name in vain; or bringing yourself to a happy place." *https://ccel.org/ccel/edersheim/lifetimes/lifetimes.ix.ix.htm.l*
—   "Doing any of the above could land you a "nezifah" one-day ban from the community. You retire to your house, speak little, and feel remorse.
—   "A niddui, a step stricter, is a week-long censure in which no one but your family may associate with you, or even sit within four cubits (six feet) of you.
    www.jta.org/jewniverse/2018/three-great.
    "Rebuked for seven days, rejected for 30 days, and treated as a dead person."
—   Matthew 18:17; 1 Corinthians 5:1– 13, 5:5; Titus 3:10; Matthew 18:17.

Rodney F. Price, D.Min.

John 9:23 <u>Therefore</u> said his parents, he is of age; ask him.

- Therefore – διὰ τοῦτο – through this

John 9:24 Then again called they the man that was blind, and said unto him, Give God the <u>praise</u>: we know that this man is a sinner.

- praise – δόξαν – glory
  Robertson's Word Pictures www.studylight.org/commentaries/eng/rwp/john.html,

John 9:25 He answered and said, Whether if. he be a <u>sinner</u> or no, I know not: one thing I know, that, whereas I was blind, now I see.

- sinner – ἁμαρτωλός – "suggesting he did not know he was a sinner;"
  John Gill https://alkitab.sabda.org/commentary,
- blind – τυφλὸς – opaque as if smoky – *Present Participle – This is an ongoing activity in the present time of the speaker.*
- "Being blind, I now see."
  Robertson's Word Picture www.studylight.org/commentaries/eng/rwp/john.html,

John 9:26 Then said they to him again, What <u>did</u> he to thee? How opened he thine eyes?

- did – εποιησεν – to make or do – *Aorist Act. Ind. – A point-in-time activity.*
- opened – ηνοιξεν – *Aorist Act. Ind. – A point-in-time activity.*

John 9:27 He answered them, I have told you already, and ye did not hear: wherefore would ye hear it again? will ye also be his disciples?

- "Negative answer formally expected."
  Robertson's Word Pictures www.studylight.org/commentaries/eng/rwp/john.htm.l
- "of what avail would it be? Or what purpose can be answered by it?"
  John Gill www.studylight.org/commentaries/eng/geb/john-9.htm.l

John 9:28 Then <u>they</u> <u>reviled</u> him, and said, Thou art his disciple; but we are Moses' disciples. – reviled – ἐλοιδόρησαν – *Aorist Act. – A point-in-time activity.*

- "Is to wound a man as with an accursed sting."
  Vincent's Word Studies https://www.studylight.org/commentaries/eng/vnt/john.html,

    –   "All Orthodox rabbis so claimed."
                       Robertson's Word Pictures /www.studylight.org/commentaries/eng/rwp/john.html,

John 9:29 We know that God spake unto Moses: as for this fellow,we <u>know</u> not from whence he is.

    –   know – οἴδαμεν – information and not by experience – *Perfect Tense – A completed action with continuing effects at a point in time.*
    –   "This fellow" – τοῦτον – These Pharisees neither knew nor cared.
                       Robertson's Word Pictures www.studylight.org/commentaries/eng/rwp/john.html,

John 9:30 The man answered and said unto them, Why herein is a <u>marvelous</u> thing, that ye know not from whence he is, and yet he hath opened mine eyes.
John 9:21-34 Is omitted

Jesus Rebukes the Pharisees.
John 9:35–38 The Defense & Care.
John 9:35 Jesus heard that they had cast him out; and when he had found him, he said unto him, Dost thou believe on the Son of God?

    –   cast him out – not excommunication, but physically.
    –   Son – Υἱὸν – He is positioned as a legal son.
    –   A direct Messianic claim.

John 9:36 He answered and said, Who is he, Lord, <u>that</u> I might believe on him?

    –   that – ἵνα – in-order-that
    –   might believe – πιστεύσω – *Aorist Act. Subj. – A potential point-in-time activity.*

John 9:37 And Jesus said unto him, Thou hast both <u>seen</u> him, and it is he that talketh with thee.

    –   seen – ἑώρακας – and continue to see – *Perfect Tense – A completed action with continuing effects at a point in time.*

John 9:38 And he said, Lord, I believe. And he worshipped him.

    –   believe – πιστεύω – believing – *Present – This is an ongoing activity in the present time of the speaker.*

John 9:39 – 41 The purpose of the light – to expose sin.

John 9:39 And Jesus said, For <u>judgment</u> I am come into this world, that they which see not might see; and that they which see might be made blind.

- judgment – κρίμα – to shift grain
- *John 3:17 "For God sent not his Son into the world to condemn the world"*
- Judging will be at His second coming at the Great White Throne.
- Signs – John 2:18, 6:30.

John 9:40 And some of the <u>Pharisees</u> which were with him heard these words, and said unto him, Are we <u>blind</u> also?

- The blindness of the Pharisees.
- Signs – John 2:18, 6:30.

John 9:41 Jesus said unto them, <u>If</u> ye were blind, ye should have no sin: but now ye say, We see; therefore your sin remaineth.

- If – <u>εἰ</u> – 2nd class conditional – contrary-to-facts. See Jeremiah 2:35.

John 10:1-42 This chapter does not directly deal with the Tabernacle areas or furniture. The topics discussed by Jesus.

- The Good Shepherd lays down his life.
- The Holy Spirit.
- Feast of Chanukkah.
- The rejected Shepherd and the true Sheep.

John 11:1-16 Omitted

John 11:1 I Am the Good Shepherd.

American culture has told us and countless other boys and young men that crying is not manly. Men are supposed to be tough. Crying is for wimps who cannot take the pain. Caring enough to cry—whether out of sadness, joy, or pain is associated with femininity weakness."

www.yourotherbrothers.com/2017/08/10/okay-men-cry.

"It is profoundly human to find ourselves in tears. Not only is it a normal human response to suffering, but it is also a Christ-like response to our pain. Jesus identifies himself as the Good Shepherd – someone who takes care of the sheep. We might not love the idea of being compared to sheep because they are not very bright animals. However, there is much power in this picture of Jesus as our shepherd. If it matters to us, it matters to Jesus. If it breaks our heart, it breaks His heart. God hears and responds to the cries of His people (Psalm 20:1). A shepherd in those days was both a leader and a caretaker."

Unknown Source

John 11:12-16 Omitted

John 11:17– 40 The Context of the raising of Lazarus.

- Lazarus, whose name means in Hebrew, "My God is my help."
- Jerusalem Talmud: "For the first three days after death, the soul floats above the body, thinking that it will return to the body. When the soul sees the body, that the appearance of the face has changed, it leaves the body and goes Its way."

Jerusalem Talmud Yebamot 16:3-PD.
https://www.sefaria.org/texts/Talmud/Yerushalmi,

- "When Lazarus finally is resurrected, a very important point emerged is not something that Jesus does. It is something that Jesus is." *Unknown Source*

— According to St. Epiphanios of Cyprus (367-403), Lazarus was thirty years old when he rose from the dead, and then went on to live another 30 years following his resurrection. Another tradition says that Lazarus fled the anger of the Jews and took refuge at Kition on Cyprus around 33 AD.

https://cmc-terrasanta.org/en/media/visit-to-cyprus/24946/from-jerusalem-to- cyprus:-the-island-of-barnabas,-paul,-lazarus-the-maritime-route-of-the-firs- Christians.
https://www.bibletools.org/../ID/5452/Lazarus.htm.

John 12:1– 34

    The anointing for Jesus' burial on the 9th of Nisan, Thursday. This occurs in the city of Bethany, in the home of Simon.

John 12:35 Then Jesus said unto them, Yet a <u>little</u> <u>while</u> is the <u>light</u> with you. Walk <u>while</u> ye have the light <u>lest</u> darkness come upon you: for he that walketh in darkness knoweth not whither he goeth.

- little while – μικρότερος – A very short time. – light – φῶς – to shine
- They are at risk of being left in the darkness. (John 12:35).
- while – You are able to receive me as the Messiah [John **8:12;** John 9:5].
- lest – that no – *ινα μη John Gill https://alkitab.sabda.org/commentary.*

John 12:36 <u>While</u> ye have, light believe in the light, <u>that</u> ye <u>may</u> <u>be</u> the <u>children</u> of <u>light</u>. These things spake Jesus, and departed, and did hide himself from them.

- While – Therefore "don't wait."
- that – *ινα* – in-order-that
- ye may – ἕως – To cause to be what God intends.
- children – υἱός – They are legal sons by position.
- Be children of light in contrast to Luke 16:.

John 12:46 I am <u>come</u> a light into the world, that whosoever believeth on me <u>should not abide</u> in darkness.

- come – εληλυθα of ἔρχομαι – *Aorist Act. – A point-in-time* activity,
- should not abide – μεινη – *Aorist Subjunctive – A point-in-time activity imagined/ wished.*

These chapters are omitted and not Tabernacle related.

John 13:1–17 The lesson on being a servant.
John 14:1–15 A prepared place with prayer privileges.
John 14:6 – I am the way, the truth, and the life.
John 15:1–11 The vine and branches, *I am the true vine.*
John 16: The Holy Spirit is the reliable replacement.

The Altar of Incense.

John 17: The Altar of Incense – The High Priestly Prayer of Jesus.
The Altar of Incense is placed on the Holy Place before the veil to the Holy of Holies.

> *Exodus 30:1 And thou shalt make an altar to burn incense upon: of shittim wood shaltt thou make it.*

> *"If we knew we were about to die, what would be on our minds? It is a scary thought, but most people would probably become consumed with the coming pain, a curiosity about the afterlife, and regrets of things we failed to accomplish."*
>
> *Unknown Source*

John records for us one of Jesus' prayers. With a sinking weight on His chest, Jesus prays, "Neither pray I for these alone, but for them also which shall believe on me through their word; That they all may be one; as thou, Father, art in me, and I in thee, that they also may be one in us: that the world may believe that thou hast sent me." (17:20– 21).

Jesus is about to be arrested and executed, but He takes the time to pray for His friends and followers. With a mind full of distractions, Jesus prayed for comfort for the people He loved. Notice for whom else He prayed. He mentioned, "those who will believe. Two years ago, Jesus, in a garden, prayed for us.

Let that sink in. Jesus prayed for us on His way to the cross. We will never be able to understand God's heart for us, but this should give us a little glimpse. We were on His mind even with His murder around the corner."   *Edited Unknown Source*

"Its material was to be like that of the ark of the testimony, but its dimensions very small."
        Jamieson, Fausset, and Brown https://www.blueletterbible.org/Comm/jfb/Jhn/Jhn_000.cfm.

Exodus 30:6 And thou shalt put it before the vail that is by the ark of the testimony, before the mercy seat that is over the testimony, where I will meet with thee.
        Revelation 8:3–4 Here we find incense connected with prayer.

John 17:1– 26 The Place of Christ's High Priestly Prayer.

"The gold altar of incense represents the intercession and the memorial of Jesus. While the golden lamp stand was to burn perpetually, the Bread of the Presence was to be replaced every Sabbath. The incense was to be burning every morning and evening. The blood applied to this altar on the Day of Atonement. Jesus is our mediator, according to 1st Timothy and Hebrew." *Alfred Edersheim's The High Priestly Prayer of Jesus.*

"In this prayer, Jesus acknowledges the fact that God gave him "authority over all people." Jesus has the authority to give us life! Moreover, we know what kind of person he is compassionate and willing to give life to anyone who comes to him. All we need to do is ask for it. It is His to give. To give us life is why Jesus came. This prayer stands at the center of our faith and reflects the character of God – that is, love. 1Corinthians 13:. God is love, and his Son loved us all the way unto death and through it to bring us into full life on the other side. This is for God's glory, and this is Jesus' glory. This glory is our salvation. What has been given by God through Christ our Savior that we can give to others?"
        Edited Unknown Source

John 17:1–5 Christ prays for Himself and for the disciples.

— Jesus' habit of praying.

- See Matthew 11:25; Mark 1:35; 6:46; Luke 3:21; 5:16; 6:12; 9:18, Luke 23:34, 23:46; John 11:41; 12:27.
- He prayed here for himself and for the disciples and for all believers.

John 17:1 These words spake Jesus, and lifted his eyes in. to heaven, and said, Father, the hour is come; glorify thy Son, that thy Son also may glorify thee.

- lifted up – ἐπῆρε – *Aorist Part.* – *A point-in-time activity.*
- glorify – *Aorist Imperative* – *A point-in-time activity, a command.*
- into – εἰς – into
- thy Son – υἱόν – A legally positioned son.
- glorify – *Aorist Act.* – *A point-in-time activity.*

John 17:2 As thou hast given him power over all flesh, that so that. he should give life to as many as thou hast given him.

- power – ἐξουσίαν – authority – eternal – αἰώνιον ageless. "without beginning and end."
  Thayer's Greek Lexicon https://www.biblestudytools.com/lexicons/greek,
- life – ζωὴν – intensive, unchanged – *Aorist* – *A point-in-time activity.*
- Note the difference. – life – βίος – Is extensive biological life.

John 17:3 And this is life eternal, that they might know knowledge by experience. thee the only true God, and Jesus Christ, whom thou hast sent.

- sent – A point-in-time activity.
- life – ζωή – intensive and unchanged
- know – γινώσκωσι – Is knowledge by experience.
- only true God. The phrase is only here and in 1:17.
- sent – ἀπέστειλας – A messenger sent with a message.

John 17:4 I have glorified thee on the earth: I have finished the work which thou gavest me to do.

- glorified – having glorified – ἐδόξασ – *Aorist Act.* – *A point-in-time activity.*
- on – ἐπὶ – upon
- finished – having finished – ἐτελείωσα – *Aorist Act.* – *A point-in-time activity.*
- to – ἵνα – in-order-that

John 17:5 And now, O Father, <u>glorify</u> thou me <u>with</u> thine own self with the glory which I <u>had</u> with thee <u>before</u> the world was.

- glorify – δόξασόν – *Aorist – A point-in-time activity.*
- with – παρὰ – o be alongside
- I had – εἶχον – *Imperfect – A past action or state which is incomplete.*
- with – παρὰ – beside. And continue to have – *Imperfect – A past action or state which is incomplete.*
- before – πρὸ – in front of

John 17:6–19 Jesus prays for the disciples.
John 17:6 I have <u>manifested</u> thy name unto the men which thou <u>gavest</u> me out of the world: thine they were, and thou <u>gavest</u> them me; and they have <u>kept</u> thy <u>word</u>.
- manifested – ᾽εφανέρωσά – *Aorist Act. – A point-in-time activity.*
- gavest – δέδωκάς – having given – *Perfect – Completed action with continuing effects.*
- kept – ετηρήκασι – having kept – *Perfect Tense – A completed action with continuing effects.*
- word – λόγον – This is the usual word for the written Word.

John 17:7 Now they have <u>known</u> by experience. that all things whatsoever thou hast given me are of thee.

- have known – ἔγνωκαν – having known – *Perfect Tense – A completed action with continuing effects at a point in time.*
- hast given – δέδωκάς – having gave – *Perfect – A completed action with continuing effects.*

John 17:8 For I have given unto them the words spoken words. which thou gavest me; and they have received them,and have known surely that I came out from thee, and they have believed that thou didst send me.

- words – ῥήματα – This is usually the spoken word.
- from – παρὰ – from alongside.

John 17:9 I pray for them: I <u>pray</u> not for the world, but for them which thou <u>hast given</u> me; for they are thine.

- pray – ἐρωτῶ – requesting – *Present – This is an ongoing activity in the present time of the speaker.*
- hast given – δέδωκάς – *Perfect – A completed action with continuing effects.*

Rodney F. Price, D.Min.

John 17:10 And <u>all</u> things. mine are thine, and thine are mine; and I am glorified in them.

- things – ἐμὰ – Nominative plural Neuter.
- are – is. – ἐστι – *Present – This is an ongoing activity in the present time of the speaker.*
- "Christ is speaking not of things but of persons." *Gill's Exposition 17:10 (biblehub.com)*
- *"All My things are Thine and Thy things are Mine."*
  Jamison, Fausset, and Brown www.blueletterbible.org/Comm/jfb/Jhn/Jhn_000.cfm

John 17:11 And now I am no more in the world, but these are in the world, and I come to thee. Holy Father, <u>keep</u> <u>through</u> thine own name those whom thou hast given me, that they may e one, as we are.

- keep – τήρησον – *Aorist – A point-in-time activity.*
- through – ἐν – in

John 17:12 While I was with them in the world, I <u>kept</u> them in thy name: those that thou gavest me I have kept, and none of them is lost, but the <u>son</u> <u>of perdition</u>; that the scripture might be fulfilled.

- kept – ἐτήρουν – continue to guard – *Imperfect – A past action which is incomplete.*
- son of – ὁ υἱὸς – He is legally placed as a son.
- perdition – τῆς ἀπωλείας – "Ruin or loss. It means the son is marked by final loss, not annihilation, but destiny."
  Robertson's Word Pictures www.studylight.org/commentaries/eng/rwp/john17.htm.l
- Compare 2Thess. 2:3 – The Antichrist.
- See *Mark 14:21 "but woe to that man by whom the Son of man is betrayed! good were it for that man if he had never been born."*

John 17:13 And now come I to thee; and these things I am <u>speaking</u> in the <u>world</u>, <u>that</u> they might have my joy <u>fulfilled</u> in themselves.

- speak – λαλῶ – speaking – *Present – This is an ongoing activity in the present time of the speaker.*
- world – κόσμῳ – Not the planet.
- that – ἵνα – in-order-that
- fulfilled – πεπληρωμένην – *Perfect Pass. Part. – A completed action with continuing effects.*

John 17:14 I have given them thy <u>word</u>; and the world hath <u>hated</u> them, because they are not of the world, even as I am not <u>of</u> the world.

- word – λόγον – Usually refers to the written Word.
- hated – εμισησεν – *Aorist Act. – A point-in-time activity.*
- of – ἐκ – out of

John 17:15 I <u>pray</u> not that thou shouldest take them out of the world, but that thou shouldest keep them <u>from</u> the <u>evil</u>.

- pray – ἐρωτῶ – praying – *Present – This is an ongoing activity in the present time of thespeaker.*
- from – ἐκ – out of
- evil – πονηροῦ – *Adj. Sing. Masc.*
- Therefore, "the evil One."

John 17:16 They are not <u>of</u> the world, even as I am not <u>of</u> the world.

- of – ἐκ – out of

John 17:17 <u>Sanctify</u> them <u>through</u> thy truth: thy <u>word</u> is truth.

- Sanctify – ἁγίασον – to make holy – *Aorist Imperative – A point in time command.*
- through – ἐν – in
- word – λόγος – Usually, the written Word.

John 17:18 As thou hast <u>sent</u> me into the world, even so have I also <u>sent</u> them into the world.

- sent – ἀπέστειλας – *Aorist Act. – A point-in-time activity.*

John 17:19 And for their sakes I <u>sanctify</u> myself, that they also might be <u>sanctified</u> <u>through</u> the truth.

- sanctify – ἁγιάζω – *Present – This is an ongoing activity in the present time of the speaker.*
- sanctified – ἡγιασμένοι – *Perfect Pass. Part. – Completed action with results.*
- through – ἐν – in

John 17:20– 26 Jesus prays for all believers.

John 17:20 Neither pray I for these alone, but for them also which <u>shall believe </u>on me through their word;

- shall believe – πιστευόντων – *Future Act. Part. – The action or a state which will take place after the action of* the main verb.

John 17:21 That they all may be <u>one;</u> as thou, Father, art in me, and I in thee, that they also may be one in us that the world may <u>believe</u> that thou hast sent me.

- one – ἐν ὦσι – in us – *Present Act. Subj. – This is a potential activity in the present time of the speaker.*
- believe – πιστεύῃ – *Aorist Subj. – **A** potential point-in-time activity.*

John 17:22 And the glory which thou <u>gavest</u> me I have <u>given</u> them; that they may be <u>one,</u> even as we are <u>one</u>:

- gavest – δέδωκάς – *Perfect – A completed action with continuing effects.*
- given – δέδωκα – *Perfect Act. Ind. – A completed action with continuing effects.*
- one – ἐσμεν – *Present – This is an ongoing activity in the present time of the speaker.*
- One is the prime number # 1.

John 17:23 I in them, and thou in me, that they may be made perfect in one; and that the world may know that thou hast sent me, and hast loved them, as thou hast loved me.

- that – ἵνα – in-order-that
- made – τετελειωμένοι – *Perfect Passive Part. – A completed action with continuing effects.*
- loved – ἠγάπσας – A relationship love – ***Aorist Act**. – A point-in-time activity.*

John 17:24 Father, I <u>will</u> that they also, whom thou hast <u>given</u> me, be with me where I am; that they may behold my glory, which thou hast given me: for thou lovedst me <u>before</u> the foundation of the world.

- will – θέλω – desirous will
- hast given – κάκεῖνοι – *Perfect Pass. Part. – Completed action with continuing effects.*
- before – πρὸ – in front of, before

John 17:25 O righteous Father, the world hath not <u>known</u> thee: but I have known thee, and these have <u>known</u> that thou hast sent me.

- known – ἔγνων – to know by experience – [2]*Aorist Act. – A point-in-time activity.*
- known – ἔγνωσαν – to know by experience – [2]*Aorist Act. – A point-in-time activity.*

John 17:26 And I have declared unto them thy name and will declare it: that the love wherewith thou hast <u>loved</u> me may be in them, and I in them.

- love – ἀγάπη – A relationship love.

The Brook Cedron.

John 18:1 When Jesus had spoken these words, he went forth with his disciples over the brook
Cedron, where was a garden, into the which he entered, and his disciples.

- Cedron – Κέδρων – A dark ravine to the northeast of Jerusalem.
- brook – A winter torrent.
  Vincent's Word Studies www.studylight.org/commentaries/eng/rwp/john.htm.l.
- over – πέραν – beyond
- garden – Gethsemane?

John 18:2 And Judas also, which <u>betrayed</u> him, <u>knew</u> the place: for Jesus oft-times resorted
thither with his disciples.

- which betrayed – ὁ παραδιδοὺς – παρα + διδοὺς – alongside.
- knew – ἤδει εἴδω. – To know intellectually

John 18:3 Judas then, having received a b<u>and</u> <u>of</u> <u>men</u> and <u>officers</u> from the chief priests And
Pharisees cometh thither with lanterns and torches and weapons.

- band of men – τὴν σπεῖραν
- The men of the Roman garrison presently dwelling in the tower of Antonia.
- officers – ὑπηρέτας – Men sent from the Sanhedrim **of** 70 men and the High Priest.

John 18:4 Jesus therefore, knowing all things that <u>should</u> <u>come</u> upon him, went forth, and said
unto them, Whom seek ye?

– should come – τὰ ἐρχόμενα – that <u>are</u> coming – *Present Middle Part. – This is an ongoing activity in the present time of the speaker.*

John 18:5 They answered him, Jesus of <u>Nazareth</u>, Jesus saith unto them, I am he. And Judas also, which betrayed him, <u>stood</u> with them.

– Nazareth – Ναζωραῖον – Nazarene
– stood – εἱστήκει – standing – continued to stand – *Imperfect – A past action or state which is incomplete.*

John 18:6 As soon then as he had said unto them, <u>I am he</u>, they went backward, and fell to the ground.

– I am, – egō eimi – To be on an equality with God.
       Vincent's Word Studies www www.studylight.org/commentaries/eng/rwp/john.htm.l
– This made them fall.
– However, Why did they step back?
– Was the deity claim of Jesus?

John 18:7 Then asked he them again, Whom seek ye? And they said, Jesus of Nazareth.

– The soldiers knew who He was.

John 18:8 Jesus answered, I have told you that I am he: if therefore ye seek me, <u>let these</u> go way:

– let these go – ἄφετε τούτους ὑπάγειν – *²Aorist Imperative – This is a punctiliar point-in-time activity, a command.*

John 18:9 That the saying might be fulfilled, which he spake, Of them which thou <u>gavest</u> me have I lost none.

– gavest – δέδωκάς – *Perf. Act. Ind.– Completed action at point-in-time with continuing results.*
    See John 6:39 "that of all which he hath given me I should lose nothing,"
    See John 17:12 "but the son of perdition."
– ἀπώλεια/perished. – ἀπωλείας – The perishing.

John 18:10 Then Simon Peter having a <u>sword</u> drew it, and smote the high priest's servant, and cut off his right ear. The servant's name was Malchus.

- sword – μάχαιραν – a short sword
- "A rule which forbade the carrying of weapons on a feast–day."
  Vincent's Word Studies www.studylight.org/commentaries/eng/rwp/john.html.
- Simon Pete and Malchus – Only in John.

John 18:11 Then said Jesus unto Peter, Put up thy the <u>sword</u> into the sheath: the cup which my father hath given me, shall I not drink it?

- sword – μάχαιραν – a short sword

Jesus Faces Annas and Caiaphas.
John 18:12 Then the band and the <u>captain</u> and officers of the Jews [Judeans]. took Jesus, and bound him,

- captain – χιλιαρχος – The commander of a thousand soldiers of the Centurions.
  www.biblehub.com/acts/21-31.html.

John 18:13 And led him away to <u>Annas</u> first; for he was father-in-law to <u>Caiaphas</u>, which was the high priest that same year.

- Annas – Ανναν – The High Priest.
- Caiaphas – Also, a High Priest – "He was the 'sagan' of the high priest."
  John Gill https://alkitab.sabda.org/commentary.

John 18:14 Now <u>Caiaphas</u> was he, which gave counsel to the Jews [Judeans] that it was that one man should die for the people.

- Caiaphas decided with the chief priests and Pharisees.
- expedient – συμφέρει – "which advice was given out of ill will and malice to Christ, and to prevent, as he thought, the people of the Jews being destroyed by the Romans." *John Gill www.biblestudytools.com/john/18-14.html.*

John 18:15 And Simon Peter <u>followed</u> Jesus, and so did <u>another</u> disciple: that disciple was known unto the high priest, and went in with Jesus into the palace of the high priest.

- followed – Ηκολούθει – was following – *Imperfect – A past action or state which is incomplete.*

- another – ἄλλος – "another of the same kind."
    - *Vine's Expository Dictionary Expository Dictionary of Old and New Testament Words.*
- Joseph of Arimathea or Nicodemus?

John 18:16 But Peter stood at the door without. Then went out that <u>other</u> disciple, which was known unto the high priest, and spake unto her that kept the door, and brought in Peter.

- other – ἄλλος – of a different kind.

Peter's First Denial.
John 18:17 Then saith the damsel that kept the door unto Peter, <u>Art</u> not thou also one of this man's disciples? He saith, I am not.

- Art not thou also – μὴ καὶ σὺ ἐκ – She has expected a negative answer.

John 18:18 And the servants and officers stood there, who had made a fire of coals; for it was cold: and they warmed themselves: and Peter stood with them, and warmed himself.

- The fire of coals – ἀνθρακιὰν – hard coal – **This is** Anthracite coal.

John 18:19-40 Jesus is Questioned by the High Priest.
John 18:19 The high priest then asked Jesus of his disciples, and of his doctrine.

- "This was Annas making a preliminary examination of Jesus probably to see on what terms Jesus made disciples whether as a mere rabbi or as Messiah."
    - *Robertson's Word Studies www.studylight.org/commentaries/eng/rwp/john*
- "Annas was the father–in–law of the high priest."
    - *F. B. Meyer biblehub.com/commentaries/ttb/john/18.htm.*
- ". . . taken from Annas to Caiaphas, who was the high priest and mouth of the Sanhedrim."
    - *John Gill www.biblestudytools.com/john/18-19.htm.1*

John 18:20 Jesus answered him, I spake openly to the world; I ever taught in the synagogue, and in the <u>temple</u>, whither the Jews [Judeans] always resort; and in secret have I said nothing.

- temple – ἱερῷ – A sacred place, that is, the entire precincts not into the Most Holy Place or Holy of Holies.
- resort – For prayer and to offer sacrifice.

John 18:21 Why askest thou me? ask them which heard me, what I have said unto them: behold, they know what I said.

- ask – ἀκηκοότας – asking – *Perfect Act. Part. – A completed action with continuing effects.*
- them – Crowds had heard Jesus debating in the temple. *John 18:22 And when he had thus spoken, one of the officers which stood by struck Jesus with the palm of his hand, saying, Answerest thou the high priest so* – stood by – παρεστηκὼς – to stand along-side
- palm – ῥάπισμα – gave a blow – *Aorist Act. – A point-in-time activity.*
- "One of the temple police who felt his importance as a protector of Annas."
  Robertson's Word Picture www.studylight.org/commentaries/eng/rwp/john-18.html.

John 18:23 Jesus answered him, If I have spoken evil, bear witness of the evil: but if well, why smitest thou me?

- If – εἰ – 1ˢᵗ class condition – It is assumed to be true.

John 18:24 Now Annas had sent him bound unto Caiaphas the high priest.

- had sent – ἀπέστειλεν – omit "had" – *Aorist – a point-in-time activity.*
- John alone gives the examination of Jesus by Annas.
- "to the full court of the Sanhedrin, under the presidency of Caiaphas."
- Jesus bound during his arrest [John 18:12]. and unbound during examination by Annas.

Peter's Second Denial.

John 18:25 And Simon Peter stood and warmed himself. They said therefore unto him, Art not thou also one of his disciples? He denied it, and said, I am not. – stood and warmed – ἑστὼς – θερμαινόμενος – *Perfect – Completed action with continuing results.*

- **See** Matt. 26:72 *"He denied with an oath, I do not know the man."*

John 18:26 One of the servants of the high priest, being his kinsman, whose ear Peter cut off, saith, Did not I see thee in the garden with him?

- servants – Including Malphus. Whose ear had been cut off and restored. See Mark 14:43-50.

Peter's Third Denial.
John 18:27 Peter then denied again: and immediately the cock crew.

- "speaks of two crowings as often happens when one cock crows."
  Robertson's Word Pictures /www.studylight.org/commentaries/eng/rwp/john.

John 18:28-40 By The World and Jesus Before Pilate

- Rome had taken away from the Jews the right to capital punishment.

John 18:28 Then led they Jesus from Caiaphas unto the <u>hall of judgment</u>: and it was early; they themselves went not into the <u>judgment hall</u>, lest they should be defiled; but that they might eat the passover.

- The hall of judgment – πραιτώριον·– The governor's court.
- Praitorion accordingly is translated in all these ways, "Praetorium," "the common hall," "the judgment hall," "the palace," "the praetorian guard."
  https://biblehub.com/topical/j/judgment_hall.htm.
- Praetorium is wherever the Roman emperor or governor, who represents the emperor, is staying or headquartered, whether it be his official residence.
- The official name for the residence of the Roman governor.
  https://www.britannica.com/quiz/us-presidential-history.
- defiled – By entering into Pilate's pagan headquarters.
- "The strict Jew would not enter a Gentile's house, nor sit on the same couch, nor eat or drink out of the same vessel. The very dust of a heathen city was defiling."
  https://biblehub.com/acts/10-28.htm.
- Passover – i.e., The evening meal of the Passover on Thursday eve.

John 18:29 <u>Pilate</u> then went out unto them, and said, What accusation bring ye against this man?

- Pilate went out over the pavement in front of his palace. See John 19:13.

John 18:30 They answered and said unto him, If he were not a malefactor, we would not have delivered him up unto thee.

- If – εἰ – *2ⁿᵈ class condition and is assumed to be untrue.*

John 18:31 Then said Pilate unto <u>them</u>, take ye him, and judge him according to your law. The <u>Jews</u> [Judeans] therefore said unto him, It is not lawful for us to put any man to death:

- them – The Judeans
- John 7:1. – John 7:25
- Crucifixion was not a Jewish punishment; only Rome had the authority.

John 18:32 That the saying of Jesus might be fulfilled, which he spake, signifying what death he should die.

- "This could only be carried into effect by order of the governor."
    Jamieson, Fausset, and Brown www.blueletterbible.org/Comm/jfb/Jhn/Jhn_000.cfm.

John 18:33 Then Pilate entered into the judgment hall <u>again</u>, and called Jesus, and said unto him, Art thou the King of the Jews? [Judeans].

- again – Jesus goes back to the palace.
- Did Pilate speak Aramaic or Greek?

John 18:34 Jesus answered him, Sayest thou this thing of thyself, or did <u>others</u> tell it thee of me?

- *"That he was the king of the Jews." John Gill https://alkitab.sabda.org/commentary.*
- others tell – εἶπο περὶ – **Aorist Act**. – A point-in-time activity.

John 18:35 Pilate answered, Am I a <u>Jew</u> [Judeans]? Thine own nation and the Chief priests have delivered thee unto me: what hast thou done?

- Am I a Jew?
- Of the tribe in Judea?
- chief priests – ἀρχιερεῖς –The Priests of the Sanhedrin.

John 18:36 Jesus answered, My kingdom is not <u>of</u> this world: if my kingdom were <u>of</u> this world then would my servants <u>fight</u>, that I should not be delivered to the Jews but now is my kingdom not from hence.

- of – ἐκ – out of
- fight – ἠγωνίζοντο – *Imperfect – A past action or state which is incomplete.*
- fight – "would now be striving."
    Vincent's Word Studies www.studylight.org/commentaries/eng/rwp/john.html.

John 18:37 Pilate therefore said unto him, Art thou a <u>king</u> then? Jesus answered, Thou sayest that I am a king. To this end was I born, and for this cause came I into the world, that I should bear witness unto the truth. Every one that is of the <u>truth</u> heareth my voice.

- king – βασιλεὺς – A king over people, not over a territory.
- the truth – τῆς ἀληθείας – Absolute truth

John 18:38 Pilate saith unto him, What is <u>truth</u>? And when he had said this, he went out again unto the Jews [Judeans]. and saith unto them, I find in him no fault at all.

- truth – generic truth – Lacks the definite article, therefore generic truth.

John 18:39 But ye have a custom, that I should release unto you one at the passover: will ye therefore that I release unto you the <u>King</u> of the Jews? [Judeans]

- King of the Jews [Judeans] – βασιλέα τῶν Ἰουδαίων – Over people and not a territory.

John 18:40 Then cried they all again, saying, Not this man, but Barabbas. Now Barabbas was a <u>robber</u>.

- robber – λῃστής
- ". . . possibly the leader of the band to which the two robbers belonged who were crucified with Jesus."
  Robertson's Word Pictures www.studylight.org/commentaries/eng/rwp/john.

The Ark of the Covenant.
John 19: Into the Holy of Holies – Jesus is Delivered to Be Crucified.

Exodus 5:18– 20 "And you shall make two cherubim of gold; of hammered work you shall make them at the two ends of the <u>mercy seat</u>. "Make one cherub at one end, and the other cherub at the other end; you shall make the cherubim at the two ends of it of one piece with the mercy seat. "And the cherubim shall stretch out their wings above, covering the mercy seat with their wings, and they shall face one another; the faces of the cherubim shall be toward the mercy seat that one man should die for the people, and that the whole nation perish not.

"Some phrases take on different meanings as we go through life. "We are moving." "I will miss you" And "I love you." This passage speaks of the horrific crucifixion of Christ. Jesus was a carpenter who had driven many nails into wood throughout His lifetime. Now, nails are driven into His own hands. Ultimately, Jesus is nailed to His wooden cross made up of trees He created. He is nailed to the cross around 9 a.m., and now it was getting close to 3 a.m. He was up there, beaten and bloodied. He was struggling to keep His breath, and He took a quick drink to clear out His throat and muster the strength to exclaim, "It is finished!" John 19:30. In the ancient context, this phrase adds commonly used in referring to debt– there are millennia– old documents where this slogan is stamped on the bottom. When Jesus said, "It is finished," He said, "It is over; it is paid in full." He did not just mutter these words: this was His victory exclamation. With that battle cry, Jesus announced that He abolished anything and everything that was getting in the way of Him and the people He loves. When Jesus said, "It is finished," we were on His mind. We tend to give much power to our shortcomings and failures, but only good news! There is unimaginable power in the name of Jesus. We must never grant power to our sin, shame, and struggles because Jesus said it is paid in full. Do not live as if it does not matter."   *Edited Unknown Source,*

John 19:1– 12 The Entrance of the Lamb.

The Faultless Lamb is made sin for us. He is not a sinner like ***us.***

John 19:1 – 12 The Entrance of the Lamb.

John 19:1 Then Pilate therefore took Jesus and <u>scourged</u> him.

- to flog was a standard penalty. – 2 Cor. 11:23– 5
- "Pilate did not scourge Jesus."
     Robertson's Word Pictures www.studylight.org/commentaries/eng/rwp/john.
- He simply ordered it done – "scourges, called scorpions, leather thongs tipped with leaden balls or spikes."
     Vincent's Word Studies www.studylight.org/commentaries/eng/rwp/john.html.
- "The wisdom of the flesh chooses the least of two evils, but God curses that wisdom."
     https://www.studylight.org/commentaries/eng/gsb/john-19.html.

John 19:2 And the soldiers platted a <u>crown</u> of thorns, and put it on his head, and they put on him a purple robe.

- crown – στέφανον – Steven's crown.
- *1 Peter 5:4 And when the chief Shepherd shall appear, ye shall receive a crown of glory that fadeth not away.*
- *"It is the crown of victory in the games; of military valor; the marriage wreath, or the festal garland, woven of leaves or made of gold in imitation of leaves."*
     Vincent's Word Studies www.studylight.org/commentaries/eng/rwp/john.html.

John 19:3 And said, Hail, King of the Jews [Judeans] *and they <u>smote</u> him with their hands.*

- smote – εδιδουν – *Imperfect – A past action or state which is incomplete.*
- "they kept on giving him slaps with their hands."
Robertson's Word Pictures www.biblestudytools.com
- Scourging and Crucifixion in Roman Tradition, Scourging was legal for Roman executions, and only women, Roman senators. and soldiers are exempted.
www.biblicalarchaeology.org/daily/biblical.

John 19:4 Pilate therefore went forth again, and saith unto them, Behold, I <u>bring</u>. Him forth to <u>you</u> that ye may know that I find [ing]. *<u>No fault</u> in him.*

- "I bring" – Pilate leads Jesus out of the palace.
- "to you – to the Sanhedrin – "no fault" See also John 8:38.

John 19:5 Then came. Jesus forth, wearing. the crown of thorns, and the purple robe. And Pilate saith unto them, <u>Behold the man.</u>

- Ecce Homo! Behold the man! *Latin Vulgate translation. https://vulgate.org.*

John 19:6 When the <u>chief priests</u> therefore and <u>officers</u> saw him, they cried out saying, Crucify him, crucify him. Pilate saith unto them, Take ye him, and crucifying. him: for I find no fault in him.

- The Temple leaders – Pharisees and Sadducees consisted of a Party of high priests are in charge of the Temple in Jerusalem.
- Pilate has declared him innocent three times. **See** John 8:38; 19:4.

John 19:7 The <u>Jews</u> [Judeans] *answered him, We have a law, and by <u>our law</u> he ought to die, because he <u>made</u> himself the <u>Son</u> of God.*

- Jews – Ἰουδαῖοι – [Judeans]
- Lev. 20:2-;27 – death by stoning.
- Note the lack of a definite article before "Son."
- our law – νόμον – Law of the Sadducees.
- "himself the Son of God." – Matt. 26:63-64; Luke 22:70 ; John 10:36.
- Son – υἱός – He positioned himself as a legal son of God.

John 19:8– 12 The submission of the Lamb.
John 19:8 When Pilate therefore heard that saying, he was the more afraid;

- "more afraid;" because of his wife's message.
- A phobia – ἐφοβήθη – An extreme or irrational fear
- Of what?

John 19:9 And went again into the judgment hall, and saith unto Jesus, Whence art thou? But Jesus gave him no answer.

- Question relating not to His mission, but His origin.
- Pilate already knew that Jesus was from Galilee, according to Luke 23:6.
- "who were his ancestors" *Gill's Exposition19:9 (biblehub.com).*

John 19:10 Then saith Pilate unto him, Speakest thou not unto me? knowest thou not that I have power to crucify thee, and have power to release thee?

- Pilate thinks that Jesus is showing contempt for the court.
- authority – ξουσίαν

John 19:11 Jesus answered, Thou couldest have no power at all against me, except it were given thee from above: therefore Caiapha he that delivered me unto thee hath the greater sin.

- Caiaphas represents the Jewish Sanhedrin.

John 19:12 And from thenceforth Pilate sought to release him: but the Jews cried out, saying, If thou let this man go, thou art not Caesar's friend: whosoever maketh himself a king speaketh against Caesar.

- sought – ζήτει – *Imperfect – A past action or state which is incomplete.*
- He made repeated attempts.
- if – ἐὰν – *3rd class condition of an assumed probability.*

John 19:13 – 42 The Crucifixion, Death, and the piercing of Christ.
See John 2:29 The next day John [The Baptist] *seeth Jesus coming unto him, and saith, Behold the Lamb of God, which taketh away the sin of the world.*

John 19:13 – 15 The Passover Lamb is Slain.

John 19:13 When Pilate therefore heard that saying, he brought Jesus forth, and sat down in the <u>judgment seat</u>. in a place that is called the <u>Pavement</u>, but in the Hebrew, <u>Gabbatha</u>.

- "Pilate's time for playing with the situation is gone; now the situation plays with him, he said, not asked, "What is truth?" Now his frightened heart, to which the emperor's favour is the supreme law of life, says, "What is justice?" *J. P. Lange https:/biblehub. com/sermons/john/19-13.htm.*
- "This was equivalent to a threat of impeachment, which we know was much dreaded by such officers as the procurators, especially of the character of Pilate or Felix. It also consummates the treachery and disgrace of the Jewish rulers, who were willing, for the purpose of destroying Jesus, to affect a zeal for the supremacy of a foreign prince."
  Jamieson, Fauset, and Brown https://biblehub.com/commentaries/john/19-13.htm.
- Judgment Seat – βῆμα – βήματος – "Bema" is the podium or platform in a synagogue from which the Torah and Prophets read to the assembly.
- A "Bema" seat raised platform for the judge outside the palace as in Acts."
  Robertson's Word Pictures www.studylight.org/commentaries/eng/rwp/john.
- "Pavement" Is an inlay with a mosaic of small tiles in the pavement.
  Cambridge English Dictionary https://dictionary.cambridge.org/us.
- Hebrew, Gabbatha, Γαββαθά – "An elevated place."

John 19:14 And it was the <u>preparation</u> of the passover, and about the sixth hour and he saith unto the Jews [Judeans], Behold your King!

- The Preparation Day was for the sacrificing of the lambs.
- Roman time – 6 a.m. – Hebrew time – 12 p.m.

John 19:15 But they cried out, Away with him, away with him, crucify him. Pilate saith unto them, Shall I crucify your <u>King</u>? The chief priests answered, We have no king but Caesar.

- The priests announced that they are governed by God and declared their allegiance to temporal and pagan power.
- King – βασιλέα – King over people and not over a certain territory.

John 19:16 – 27 The Lamb's title and the Crucifixion.

John 19:16 Then <u>delivered</u> he him therefore unto <u>them</u> to be crucified. And they took Jesus, and <u>led</u> him away.

- delivered up – παρέδωκεν – *2ⁿᵈAorist – This is a punctiliar point-in-time activity.*
- them – the Soldiers, not the Judeans.
- led – ἤγαγον – led as a "lamb to the slaughter." See Isaiah 53:7.
- *Acts 2:23 Him, being delivered by the determinate counsel and foreknowledge of God, ye have taken, and by wicked hands have crucified and slain:*
- Jewish Sanhedrin disclaimed all responsibility for their action.

John 19:17 And he <u>bearing</u> <u>his</u> cross went forth into a place called the place of a skull, which is called in the <u>Hebrew</u> <u>Golgotha</u>: גֻּלְגֹּלֶת

- bearing – βαστάζων – *Present Participle – This is an ongoing activity in present time.*
- his – αὐτοῦ – "bearing the cross for Himself." – Reflexive pronouns.
- Compare Hebrews 13:11–13, "without the camp," or "without the gate."
- Simon of Cyrene is not mentioned by John, as did Matthew and Mark.
- Hebrew – Ἑβραϊστὶ – Jewish (Chaldee) language.
- Greek – Golgotha is near Jerusalem.
- Golgotha – גֻּלְגֹּלֶת. Golgotha is an Aramaic word meaning "the place of the skull." – All four gospels testify that it was the place of Jesus' crucifixion. And when they came to a place called Golgotha which means Place of a Skull. (Matthew 27:33). *www. biblestudytools.com/dictionary/golgotha*
- The word Calvary comes from the Latin "calvaria" meaning skull . . ."
- Calvary is located northwest of the city of Jerusalem.

John 19:18 Where they <u>crucified</u> him, and two <u>others</u> with him, on either side one, and Jesus in the <u>midst</u>.

- crucified – ἐσταύρωσαν – to impale on the cross by the soldiers
- other – ἄλλους – A different kind of person. They were thieves.
- Luke 23:33, "thieves" rather than "robbers" See Matt. 7:38.
- midst – μέσος – in the middle of.
- "malefactors" – κακοῦργος – A worthless doer as in Luke 23:33.
- "expedient, to hold Him up as the worst of the three. But in this, as in many other of their doings, "the scripture was fulfilled, which saith Isa. 53:12."

Edited from Jamieson Fausset and Brown https://dictionary.cambridge.org/us/.

John 19:19 And Pilate wrote a title and put it on the cross. And the <u>writing</u> said JESUS OF NAZARETH — THE KING OF THE JEWS.

- writing – γεγραμμένον – *Perfect Pass. Part. – A completed action continuing effects.*
- John mentions the fact that Pilate wrote the inscription. And did not call Jesus the King of Israel, but of the Jews.
- Pilate – As the fifth governor of the Roman province of Judea.
- wrote – Only John tells us Pilate wrote it.

John 19:20 This title then read many of the Jews [Judeans]: for the place where Jesus was crucified was nigh to the city: and it was written in Hebrew, Greek, and Latin.

Εβραϊστί Syro – Chaldaic, Ἑλληνιστί, Ῥωμαϊστί.
OUTOS ESTIN O BASILEUS TWN IOUDAIWN
Iēsus Nazarene' s, Rēx Iūdaeōrum

- The first letter of each word forms an acrostic YHWH.
- In Hebrew, the language of the Judean Temple leadership.
- In Greek, the language of the Gentile population.
- In Latin, the legal and official language of the Roman Empire.
- "Ieusus Nazarenus Rex Iudaeorum," or "Jesus the Nazarene King of the Jews."

John 19:21 Then said the <u>chief priests</u> of the Jews [Judeans] to Pilate, Write not, The King of the Jews; but that he said, I am <u>King</u> of the <u>Jews</u>.

- chief priests – ἀρχιερεῖς – High Priest of the Temple
- King – βασιλεὺς – A king of people, and not over a territory.
- Jews – Ἰουδαίων – [Judeans] – People of Judea.

Rodney F. Price, D.Min.

John 19:22 Pilate answered, What I have written I have written.

— "a proconsul's table is his sentence, which being once read, not one letter can be the instrument of the province;"

John Gill – Apuleus and Antonine Rome: Historical Essays Roman Society and Roman Law p. 47.

John 19:23 Then the soldiers, when they had crucified Jesus, <u>took</u> his <u>garments,</u> and made four parts, to every soldier a part; and also his coat: now the coat was without <u>seam,</u> <u>woven</u> from the top throughout.

— took – ἔλαβον – "They had stripped his body, crucifying him naked."

Gill's Exposition (biblehub.com).

— garments – ἱμάτια – "The headgear, the sandals, the girdle, and the tallith or square outer garment with fringes."

Vincent's Word Studies www.studylight.org/commentaries/eng/rwp/john.html.

— seam – ἄῤῥαφος – Only ref. in N.T.
— Exodus 39:27 – Made like the High Priest's garment.
— woven – ὑφαντὸς – no needlework – Only here in N.T.
— "The normal procedure of the Romans was not to permit the burial of crucified criminals, but rather to leave their bodies exposed, foul carrion for birds and dogs, as a lasting deterrent . . ."

https://bibleinterp.arizona.edu/articles/final–days–jesus *and realities-roman–punishment–what–happened–all–those–bodies.*

John 19:24 They said therefore among themselves, Let us not rend it, but cast lots for it, whose it shall be: that the scripture might be fulfilled, which saith, They parted my <u>raiment</u> among them, and for my <u>vesture</u> they did cast lots. These things therefore the soldiers did.

— vesture – ἱματισμόν – raiment
— *Psalm 22:18 They part my garments among them, and cast lots upon my vesture.*

John 19:25 Now there <u>stood</u> <u>by</u> the cross of Jesus his mother, and his mother's sister, Mary the wife of Cleophas, and Mary Magdalene.

— stood – εἰστήκεισαν – And continued to stand. – *A completed action with continuing effects at a point in time.*
— by – παρὰ – alongside

John 19:26 When Jesus therefore <u>saw</u> his mother and the disciple standing by, whom he <u>loved</u>, he saith unto his mother, Woman, behold thy <u>son.</u>

- saw – ἰδὼν – *Aorist **Act.** – A point-in-time activity.*
- loved – ἠγάπα –A relationship love. *Imperfect – past action which is incomplete.* – son – υἱός – He is a legal son.
- Rashi's Commentary on Deut. 21 – 22 – 23. "Our Rabbis said: All who are stoned by the court. must after words. be hanged, for the verse 23. says, "a hanging human corpse is a blasphemy of God." Thus, we find that the sin of blasphemy is connected with hanging." *https://www.sefaria.org/Sanhedrin.45b.*

John 19:27 Then saith he to the disciple, <u>Behold</u> thy mother! And from that hour that disciple took her unto his own home.

- Behold – ἴδε – to command – *Aorist Imperative – A point-in-time activity, a command.*

The Death of the Lamb.
John 19:28 After this, Jesus knowing that all things were now <u>accomplished</u>, that the scripture might be <u>fulfilled</u>, saith, I thirst.

- accomplished – τετέλεσται – *Perfect Pass. Subj. – A potential point-in-time activity.*
- fulfilled – τελειόω

John 19:29 Now there was set a vessel full of vinegar: and they filled a spunge with vinegar, and put it upon hyssop, and put it to his mouth.

- vinegar – ὄξους – "Not vinegar drugged with myrrh;" See Mark 15:23. 'and gall."
- "Matt. 7:3 "which Jesus had refused just before the crucifixion."
  Robertson's Word Picture www.studylight.org/commentaries/eng/rwp/john.
- hyssop – ὑσσώπῳ – "The hyssop reed was not more than three or four feet."
  Vincent's Word Studies www.studylight.org/commentaries/eng/rwp/john.html.

John 19:30 When Jesus therefore had received the vinegar, he said, It is <u>finished</u>: and he bowed his head, and gave up the ghost.

- This is the only time in this Gospel where Jesus drinks.
- finished – τετέλεσται – achieved, finished – *Perfect Pass. – A completed action with continuing effects.*

> *"Nothing to pay? – no, not one wit:*
> *Nothing to do – no, not a bit;*
> *All that needs to do or pay,*
> *Jesus has done it in His own blessed way."*
> H. A. Ironside
> *https://hymnary.org/text/nothing_to_pay_ah_nothing_to_pay*

- gave up – παρέδωκε – yield up – "Father, into thy hands," Luke 4:46.
- ghost – πνεῦμα – spirit

Jesus' Side is Pierced.

John 19:31 The Jews [Judeans]. therefore, because it was the <u>preparation</u>, that the bodies should not <u>remain</u> upon the cross on the sabbath day, for that sabbath day was an high day. besought Pilate that their legs might be broken, and that they might be taken away.

- preparation – παρασκευη – The day before the Sabbath was a "high day" not the seventh day Sabbath.
- Should not remain upon – per Mosaic Law – See Deut. 21:22, 23.
- "Thus, we find that the sin of blasphemy is connected with hanging, and a blasphemer is punished by stoning. Consequently, our Rabbis taught that all those stoned must be hanged." *Rashi's Commentary on Talmud – Devarim – Sanhedrin 45b.*

John 19:32 Then came the soldiers, and brake the legs of the first, and of the other which was crucified with him.

- brake – κατέαξαν – only by John. – "This *crurifragium*, leg– breaking, striking of the legs with a heavy mallet in order to expedite death." *Vincent's Word Studies www. studylight.org/commentaries/eng/rwp/john.html.*

John 19:33 But when they came to Jesus, and saw that he was <u>dead</u> already, they brake not his legs:

- dead – τεθνηκότα – natural death – *Perfect – Completed action with continuing effects.*
- So then, Jesus died before the robbers. He died of a broken heart.

John 19:34 But one of the soldiers with a spear pierced his side, and forthwith came there out blood and water.

- ". . . the spear pierced the left side of Jesus near the heart and that Jesus had died literally of a broken heart since blood is mixed with water." *Robertson's Word Pictures www. studylight.org/commentaries/eng/rwp/john-19.htm.l.*
- *Revelation 5:6 . . . stood a Lamb as it had been slain,*
- *Isaiah 53:10. Yet it pleased the LORD to bruise him; he hath put him to grief: when thou shalt make his soul an offering for sin, he shall see his seed, he shall prolong his days, and the pleasure of the LORD shall prosper in his hand.*
- *Hebrews 9:26 – 28 For then must he often have suffered since the foundation of the world: but now once in the end of the world hath he appeared to put away sin by the sacrifice of himself. And as it is appointed unto men once to die, but after this the judgment: So Christ was once offered to bear the sins of many; and unto them that look for him shall he appear the second time without sin unto salvation.*
- *Hebrews 10:9 – 12 Then said he, Lo, I come to do thy will, O God. He taketh away the first, that he may establish the second. By the which will we are sanctified through the offering of the body of Jesus Christ once for all. And every priest standeth daily ministering and offering oftentimes the same sacrifices, which can never take away sins: But this man, after he had offered one sacrifice forsins forever, sat down on the right-hand of God.*

"Lifted up was He to die.
'It is finished' was His cry.
Now in Heaven, exalted high,
Hallelujah! What a Saviour!"
https://www.hymnal.net/en/hymn/h/108

John 19:35 And he that saw it bare record, and his record is true: and he knoweth that he saith true, that ye might believe.

- he – John was there and saw this event.
- saw – ἑωρακὼς – continued to see – *Perfect – Completed action with continuing effects.*

John 19:36 For these things were done, that the scripture should be fulfilled, A bone of him shall not be <u>broken</u>.

- broken – συντριβήσεται – crushed
- *Psalm 34:20 He keepeth all his bones: not one of them is broken.*

John 19:37 And again another scripture saith, They shall look on him whom they pierced. –pierced – ἐξεκέντησαν – *Aorist Act. – A point-in-time activity. – Zech. 12:10 . . . and they shall look upon me whom they have pierced . . .,*

- *Matt. 7:51 And, behold, the veil of the temple was rent in twain from the top to the bottom; and the earth did quake, and the rocks rent; Luke 4:45.*
- "It was getting close to 3 PM. He was up there, beaten and bloodied. He was struggling to keep His breath, and He took a quick drink to clear out His throat and muster the strength to exclaim, "It is finished!" In the ancient context, this phrase is commonly used in referring to debt– there are millennia– old documents where this slogan is stamped on the bottom. When Jesus said, "It is finished," He was saying, "It is over; it is paid in full." This was His victory exclamation. With that battle cry, Jesus announced that He abolished anything and everything that was getting in the way of Him and the people He loves. When Jesus said, "It is finished." we were on His mind." *Edited Unknown Source.*

The Ark of the Covenant.

John 20:1– 30 The Return to the Holy Place.

John 20:1 The <u>first</u> <u>day</u> of cometh Mary Magdalene early, when it was yet <u>dark</u>, unto the sepulchre, and seeth the stone <u>taken</u> <u>away</u> from the sepulchre.

- first – σαββάτων – Became the new beginning of weeks, "The Lord's Day."
- A Hebrew idiom, "day one of the week."
- dark – Before 6 A.M.
- taken away – ἡρμένον to – lift, by implication to take up or away.

John 20:2 Then she runneth, and cometh to Simon Peter, and to the other disciple, whom Jesus <u>loved</u>, and saith unto them, <u>They</u> have <u>taken</u> <u>away</u> the Lord out of the sepulchre, and we know not where they have laid him.

- loved – ἐφίλει – personal affection – of φιλέω – *Imperfect – A past action incomplete.*
- they – They are not identified – Third person plural.
- taken away – ἦραν – *1ˢᵗ Aorist Act. – A point-in-time activity.*

John 20:3 Peter, therefore, <u>went forth,</u> and that <u>other</u> <u>disciple,</u> and came <u>to</u> the sepulchre.

- went forth – εξηλθεν
- another disciple, A self– styled name John calls himself.

John 20:4 So <u>they</u> <u>ran</u> both together: and the other disciple did outrun Peter, and came first to the sepulchre.

- to – εἰς – into

- they – Peter and John.
- ran – ἔτρεχον – ran –

John 20:5 And he <u>stooping</u> <u>down</u>, and looking in, saw the linen clothes <u>lying</u>; yet went he not in.

- he – John
- stooping down – παρακύψας – to bend beside – *Aorist Act. – A point-in-time activity.*
- lying – κείμενα – to lie outstretched – *Present Act. Part. – This is an ongoing activity in the present time of the speaker.*
- "Jesus was. loosed from the burial cloths, so that they collapsed placed."
  Jewish N.T. Commentary https://kifakz.github.io/eng/bible/stern/index.html.

John 20:6 Then cometh Simon Peter following him, and went into the sepulchre, and seeth the linen clothes lie,

- "If the body was removed, these clothes would have gone also."
  Robertson's Word Picture www.studylight.org/commentaries/.

John 20:7 And the <u>napkin</u>, that was about his head, not lying with the linen clothes, but <u>wrapped together</u> in a place by itself.

- napkin – σουδάριον – A sweat cloth is binding the face of a corpse.
- wrapped together – ἐντετυλιγμένον – entwine – wind up in – wrap in – together

John 20:8 Then went in also that other disciple, which came first to the sepulchre, and he <u>saw</u>, and <u>believed</u>.

- saw – εἶδε – to stare at
- believed – πίστευσεν – *Aorist Act. – A point-in-time activity.*

John 20:9 For as yet they <u>knew</u> not the scripture, that he must rise again from the dead

- knew – ἤδεισαν – factual knowledge

John 20:10 Then the disciples went away again unto their own home.

- *John has taken the mother of Jesus to his home in Ephesus.*

Jesus Appears to Mary Magdalene.

John 20:11 But Mary stood without at the sepulchre <u>weeping</u>: and as she wept, she <u>stooped</u> down, and looked into the sepulchre.

- weeping – ἔκλαιε – to sob, that is, wail aloud and continue to weep. *Imperfect – A past action or state which is incomplete.*
- stooped – to bend beside – παρακύψας

John 20:12 And seeth two angels in white sitting, the one at the head, and the other at the feet, where the body of Jesus <u>had</u> <u>lain</u>.

- Are Peter and John aware of the two angels?
- had lain – ἔκειτο – lying – *Imperfect – A past action or state which is incomplete.*

John 20:13 And they say unto her, Woman, why weepest thou? She saith unto them, Because they have taken away my Lord, and I know not where they have laid him. – Did she not see the disciples?

John 20:14 And when she had thus said, she turned herself back, and <u>saw</u> Jesus standing, and knew not that it was Jesus.

- saw – θεωρεῖ – seeing – *Present – This is an ongoing activity in the present time of the speaker.*

John 20:15 Jesus saith unto her, Woman, why weepest thou? whom seekest thou? She, supposing him to be the <u>gardener</u>, saith unto him, Sir, <u>if</u> thou have borne him hence, tell me where thou hast laid him, and I will take him away. – gardener – κηπουρός – Found only here in the N.T.

- if – εἰ – *1st class condition assumes reality.*

John 20:16 Jesus saith unto her, Mary. She turned herself, and saith unto him, <u>Rabboni</u>; which is to say, Master.

- Rabboni – ῥαββουνι – Master – Aramaic for διδάσκαλος - a Teacher.

John 20:17 Jesus saith unto her, <u>Touch</u> me not; for I am not yet <u>ascended</u> to my Father: but go to my brethren and say unto them, I ascend unto my Father, and your Father; and to my God, and your God.

Rodney F. Price, D.Min.

- Touch – ἅπτου – to attach oneself to, cling.
- ascended – ἀναβέβηκα – *Perfect Tense – A completed action with continuing effects.*
- He is still here because his activity has not been completed.
- my God – Θεόν μου – "God of me."
- **See** Mark 15:34; Rev. 3:2 and Paul's comment about Jesus in Rom. 15:6.

John 20:18 Mary Magdalene came and told the disciples that she had seen the Lord, and that he had spoken these things unto her.

- had seen – ἑώρακε – *Perfect Tense – A completed action with continuing effects.*

Jesus Appears to the Disciples.
John 20:19 Then the same day at evening, being the first day of the week, when the doors were shut where the disciples were assembled for fear of the Jews. [Judeans] came Jesus and stood in the midst, and saith unto them, Peace be unto you.

- evening – The time is from 6 to 9 p.m. John 6:16.
- first day – i.e., Saturday evening. Hebrew idiom, for the first day of the week.
- See Mark 16:2 and Luke 24:1. – "behind locked doors out of fear of the Jews."[Judeans]
  Jewish NT Commentary https://www.biblegateway.com.

John 20:20 And when he had so said, he shewed unto them his hands and his side. Then were the disciples glad when they saw the Lord.

- hands and his side – The reality of His resurrection.
- "This body, not yet glorified retained the marks of the nails and of the soldier's spear."
  Robertson's Word Pictures www.studylight.org/commentaries/eng/rwp/john20.html,

John 20:21 Then said Jesus to them again, Peace be unto you: as my Father hath sent me, even so send I you.

- so send – One of Jesus' three commissions on the mountain in Galilee.
- See Matt. 28:16– 20; 1Cor. 15:6. Mount of Olives Luke 24:44– 51; Acts 1:3– 11.
- hath sent – ἀπέσταλκέ – To send with a continuing activity. *Perfect Tense – Completed action with continuing results.*
- send – ἔμπω – sending – *Present – This is an ongoing activity in the present time of the speaker.*

John 20:22 And when he had said this, he breathed on them, and saith unto them, <u>Receive</u> ye the Holy Ghost:

- receive – λάβετε – "ye" as a group of 12 received – *Aorist – A point-in-time activity.*
- This group is not the same group as in Acts 1:15ff.

John 20:23 Whose soever sins ye <u>remit,</u> they <u>are</u> <u>remitted</u> unto them; and whose soever <u>sins</u> ye retain, they are retained.

- sins – ἀμαρτίας – remit – ἀφίενται – ". . . to us is the power and privilege of giving assurance of the forgiveness of sins by God by correctly announcing the terms of forgiveness."
  Robertson's Word Pictures www.studylight.org/commentaries/eng/rwp/john-20.htm.l
- retain – κεκράτηνται – *Perfect Pass. Ind. – A completed action with continuing effects at a point in time.*
- "The power to forgive sin belongs only to God."
  Robertson's Word Pictures www.studylight.org/commentaries/eng/rwp/john-20.htm

Jesus and Thomas.
John 20:24 But Thomas, one of the <u>twelve,</u> called <u>Didymus,</u> was not with them when Jesus came.

- The term "twelve" is applied to the group, though Judas, the traitor, is dead.
- The same expression applied to Thomas in John."
  Robertson's Word Pictures www.studylight.org/commentaries/eng/rwp/john.
- Didymus – He is a twin.

John 20:25 The other disciples therefore said unto him, We have seen the Lord. But he said unto them, <u>Except</u> I shall see in his hands the print of the nails, and put my finger into the print of the nails, and thrust my hand into his side, I will not believe.

- except – ἐὰν – 3rd class condition – uncertain fulfillment.
- not – οὐ μὴ – A double negative, therefore a positive decision.

John 20:26 And <u>after</u> eight days again his disciples were within, and Thomas with them: then came Jesus, the doors being shut, and stood in the midst, and said, Peace be unto you.

- The next Sunday evening.

Rodney F. Price, D.Min.

John 20:27 Then saith he to Thomas, Reach hither thy finger, and behold my hands; and reach hither thy hand, and thrust it into my side: and be not <u>faithless</u>, but <u>believing</u>.

- be not faithless – μὴ γίνου ἄπιστος – "stop becoming disbelieving."
- unbelieving, – but believing – ἄπιστος ἀλλὰ πιστός.

John 20:28 And Thomas answered and said unto him, My Lord and my God. – It appears that Thomas is not wholly convinced.

John 20:29 Jesus saith unto him, Thomas, because thou <u>hast</u> <u>seen</u> me, thou hast believed: blessed are they that have not seen, and yet have believed.

- hast seen – ἑώρακάς – *Perfect Tense – Completed action with continuing effects.*

The Purpose of This Book.
John 20:30 And many other <u>signs</u> truly did Jesus in the presence of his disciples, which are not written in this book.

- signs – σημεῖα – Often in this Gospel is called a miracle.

John 20:31 But these are written, that ye <u>might</u> <u>believe</u> that Jesus is the Christ, the Son of God; and that believing ye might have <u>life</u> through his name.

- might believe – πιστεύσητε – *Aorist Act. Subj. – A hypothetical point-in-time activity.*
- might have life – ζωὴν ἔχῃτ – *Present Subj. – This is an ongoing activity in the present Time of the speaker of "Hypothetical" situations.*
- "That the *future history of Christians, both in life and death, is foreknown by Christ."*
  Charles Ryle www.sermonindex.net/modules/articles/index.php?view=article&aid

John 20:31 But these are written, that ye might believe that Jesus is the Christ, the Son of God; and that believing ye might have life through his name.

"John has recorded what he has witnessed and experienced of Jesus' mission here on earth. John has written down many. However, not all of Jesus' words, teachings, and miracles (or "signs"). John states that his purpose for writing is "that you may believe." The book of John is one of the most translated books in history. Missionaries who translate the Bible into other languages often begin with the Gospel of John because it so clearly delivers the saving truth, in story form, to those who read it. John's message is much more than a story to be read and then set aside. Instead, it is aimed directly at people's hearts and promises abundant and eternal life! In believing John's message about Jesus, we are assured of God's love and forgiveness, and equipped to live as God's child.

On Wednesday, Jesus was beaten, crucified, and buried in a borrowed tomb. After that, the disciples all scattered. Fear led them to hide in terror. With all the agony of Wednesday, they could not even imagine the glory of Sunday. Jesus broke out of that borrowed grave! We often have a terrible tendency to "read the Bible backward" since we are fully aware that the resurrection is coming. Jesus' followers were not expecting it, however.

Thus, we can imagine their shock and celebration when Jesus appeared before them on the first day (John 20:19). All disciples embraced Jesus in joy, except Thomas (John 20:24). When Jesus died, it undoubtedly shook Thomas at the core. The doubting apostle was sure that Jesus was going to change the world, but then he had to watch him die a criminal's death. He gave up everything to follow Jesus, and his entire world was falling apart after the tragic events of /the crucifixion. When the disciples told him that Jesus was alive, Thomas said, "I won't believe it unless I see the nail wounds in his hands" (John 20:27). We often give Thomas a bad reputation. It is hard to believe something so glorious in the midst of the worst weekend of his life. His doubts brought him closer to the divine. The same is true for us.

Doubts are entirely natural, but our doubts must start discussions. Ultimately, those honest discussions will fuel our faith. Be open and honest about our doubts and ask Jesus to increase our faith. When we focus on our faith, our doubts slowly disappear."

Edited *www.getsemani.org/studentblog/john-20*

The Ark of the Covenant.

John 21:1– 25 Tabernacle – Holy Place – Jesus Appears to Seven Disciple. "We may be familiar with the last supper but have "we heard of the first breakfast? The Gospel of John concludes on a beach shore where Jesus cooking up breakfast for His disciples. This moment is packed full of awkward tension as Jesus focuses his attention on Peter. Just a few days earlier, Peter denied Jesus three times after Jesus' arrest. Jesus looks at Peter and asks, "Do you love me?" Not once, but three times as an echo of Peter's denial. Then, Jesus went on to say, "Follow me" (John 21:19). "Jesus, full of forgiveness, invites the disciples on a journey to follow Him. He could have quickly just said, "Peter, you messed up! What were you thinking?" However, He didn't, He extended a second chance to the denying disciple. Then, He invites him on a new adventure with Him. Wait, how can that be? Is not the ministry of Jesus ending? That is the fantastic thing about the story of Jesus. It doesn't start with a cradle or end at a cross. "This story unfolds every time a person shares the gospel with a friend, whenever we choose to show God's love in a situation that desperately needs it, or whenever we sacrifice our comforts so that someone cares for us. The invitation today is the same as it was 2,000 years ago: follow me." *Edited Unknown Source.*

John 21:1 After these things Jesus <u>shewed</u> himself again to the disciples at the sea of Tiberias; and on this wise shewed he himself. – shewed – ἐφανέρωσεν – *Aorist Act. – A point-in-time activity.*

John 21:2 Then she runneth, and cometh to Simon Peter, and to the other disciple, whom Jesus <u>loved</u>, and saith unto them, They <u>have taken away</u> the Lord out of the sepulchre, and we <u>know not</u> where they have laid him.

- loved – εφιλει – Personal affection – *Imperfect – A past action which is incomplete.*
- have taken away – ηραν – to liftup; – *Aorist Act. – A point-in-time activity.*
- know not – οιδαμεν – mentally – *Perfect Tense – Completed action with continuing results.*

John 21:3 Simon Peter <u>saith</u> unto them, I <u>go a fishing</u>. They say unto him, We also go with thee. They went forth, and entered into a ship immediately; and that night they caught nothing.

- saith – saying – λέγει – *Present – This is an ongoing activity in the present time of the speaker.*
- I go a fishing – ὑπάγω – I am going for myself. *Present Mid.– This is an ongoing activity in the present time of the speaker.*

John 21:4 But when the morning <u>was now come</u>, Jesus <u>stood</u> on the shore: but the disciples <u>knew</u> not that it was Jesus. – was now come – γενομένης – *²Aorist Participle – A point-in-time activity.*

- stood – ἵστημι – *²Aorist Act. – A point-in-time activity.* – knew – ἤδεισαν – by Information

John 21:5 Then Jesus saith unto them, Children, have ye any meat? They <u>answered</u> him NO

- answered – ἀπεκρίθησαν – *Aorist Mid. – A point-in-time activity for themselves.*

John 21:6 And he said unto them, <u>Cast</u> the net on the right side of the ship, and ye shall find. They cast therefore, and now they were not able to draw it for the multitude of fishes. – cast – βάλετε – *²Aorist Middle – A point-in-time activity for themselves.*

John 21:7 Therefore that disciple whom Jesus <u>loved</u> saith unto Peter, It is the Lord. Now when Simon Peter heard that it was the Lord, he girt his fisher's coat unto him, (for he was naked,) *and did cast himself into the sea. – loved – ἠγάπα – Imperfect – A past action or state which is incomplete.*

John 21:8 And the other disciples <u>came</u> in a little ship; (for they were not far from land, but as it were two hundred cubits, <u>dragging</u> the net with fishes. – came – ηλθον – ²Aorist Middle – A point-in-time activity for themselves.

John 21:9 As soon then as they <u>were</u> <u>come</u> to land, they saw a fire of coals there, and fish laid thereon, and bread. – were come – βλέπουσιν – To look at, to star at something.

John 21:11 Simon Peter went up, and drew the net to land full of great fishes, an <u>hundred</u> <u>and</u> <u>fifty</u> <u>and</u> <u>three</u>: and for all there were so many, yet was not the net broken.

*Concerning the Number 153.
        Jesus personally blessed 153 persons.
        They caught 153 Great fish.
        The Tabernacle has 153 Great pieces.
    The Materials of the Tabernacle.
    The Fence 60 Posts
        60 The Sockets for the posts.
        3 White fence curtains
        1 Gate entrance curtain.
        48 Boards for walls of Holy Place & Holy of Holies
    The Courtyard.
        1 Brass Altar
        2 Staves to transport when moving to follow the Lord. 1 Brass Laver– Holy Place
        1 Entrance curtain 5 Posts for the curtain
    The Holy Place
        1 Table of Shewbread/Showbread – for the visible unleavened bread.
        2 Staves to transport when moving to follow the Lord.
        1 Candlestick
        1 Altar of Incense
        2 Staves to transport when moving to follow the Lord.
    The Holy of Holies. 1 Entrance curtain 4 Posts for the curtain 4 Sockets for the posts 1 Ark of Covenant 1 Mercy Seat 1 Aaron's Rod that budded 1 Gold Pot for Manna
        2 Stones of the Law
    The Tabernacle Coverings over the Tabernacle Building. 1 White linen 1 Woven Goat's hair 1 Ram's skin dyed red 1 Badger's or Dolphin skins

John 21:12 Jesus saith unto them, <u>Come</u> and <u>dine</u>. And none of the disciples durst ask him, thou? knowing that it was the Lord. – come – dine – *Aorist Imperative – This is a punctiliar point-in-time activity, with command.*

John 21:13 Jesus then <u>cometh</u>, and <u>taketh</u> bread, and giveth them, and fish likewise. – cometh – ἔρχετα – *Pres.Mid. Ind. – This is an ongoing activity.* – taketh – λαμβανει – οψαριον – taking – *Present – This is an ongoing activity in the present time of the speaker.*

- fish – ὀψάριον – small fish – presumably salted and dried as a condiment.

John 21:14 This is now the third time that Jesus shewed himself to his <u>disciples</u>, after that he was risen from the dead. – the third time. **See** John 20:19–26. – disciples – Jesus and Peter.

John 21:15 So when they had dined, Jesus saith to Simon Peter, Simon, son of Jonas, <u>lovest</u> thou me more than these? He saith unto him, Yea, Lord; thou knowest that I <u>love</u> thee. He saith unto him, <u>Feed</u> my <u>lambs</u>.

- lovest – relationship love – ἀγαπᾷς – Present – an ongoing activity.
- love – emotional – φιλῶ – Present – an ongoing activity.
- knowest – οιδας – **Intellectually** – Perfect – *Completed action with continuing results.*
- Feed – to feed, pasture – βόσκε – Present Imperative – *This is an ongoing activity in the present time of the speaker, a command.*
- lambs – ἀρνίον – The little lambs.

John 21:16 He saith to him again the <u>second</u> time, Simon, son of Jonas, <u>lovest</u> thou me? He saith unto him, Yea, Lord; thou knowest that I <u>love</u> thee. He saith unto him, Feed my <u>sheep</u>. – lovest – ἀγαπᾷς – A relationship love.

- I love thee. – φιλῶ – emotional love
- *Feed* – ποίμαινε – Present Imperative – Ong**oing activity with a command.**
- sheep – πρόβατά

John 21:17 He saith unto him the third time, Simon, son of Jonas, lovest thou me? Peter was grieved because he said unto him the third time, <u>Lovest</u> thou me? And he said unto him, Lord, thou knowest all things; thou knowest that I love thee. Jesus saith unto him, Feed my <u>sheep</u>. – Lovest – φιλεῖς – Jesus adopts Peter's word.

- feed Present active imperative
  sheep – πρόβατά – A walking lamb.

Rodney F. Price, D.Min.

John 21:18 Verily, verily, I say unto thee, When thou wast <u>young</u>, thou girdedst thyself, and walkedst whither thou wouldest: but when thou shalt be old, thou shalt stretch forth thy hands, and another shall gird thee and carry thee whither thou wouldest not. – young – νεώτερος – a neophyte – A beginner or novice.

- old – περιεπάτεις – "whenever thou growest old"
- girdedst – ζώννυμι – girding his fisher– man's coat around himself – he being naked.

John 21:19 This spake he, signifying by what <u>death</u> he should glorify God. And when he had spoken this, he saith unto him, Follow Me . – death – θανατω – The death of the body.

Jesus and the Beloved Apostle.
John 21:20 Then Peter <u>turning about</u>, seeth the disciple whom Jesus <u>loved</u> following; which also <u>leaned</u> on his breast at supper, and said, Lord, which is he that betrayeth thee? – turning about – Ἐπιστραφεὶς – A sudden turning round. – leaned back – ἀνέπεσεν – leaned – to recline at a table, as to sit back. – loved – ἠγάπα – relational, not physical

John 21:21 Peter seeing him saith to Jesus, Lord, and what shall this this man do? – this man do? – δὲ τί – He is referring to John.

John 21:22 Jesus <u>saith</u> unto him, If I <u>will</u> that he tarry till I come, what is that to thee? follow thou me.

- saith – λέγει – saying – *Present – This is an ongoing activity in the present time of the speaker.*
- I will – θέλω – desire – *Present Subj. – This is a potential ongoing activity in the present time of the speaker.*

John 21:23 Then went this saying abroad among the brethren, that that disciple should not <u>die</u>: yet Jesus said not unto him, He shall not die; but, If I will that he tarry till I come, what is that to thee? – ἀποθνήσκει – Literally, dieth not. to die off – Present – ongoing activity. – John is the last living disciple, having survived attempts to kill him.

John 21:24 This is the <u>disciple</u> which testifieth of these things, and wrote these things: and we know that his testimony is true. – John explains that he was the unnamed disciple.

John 21:25 And there are also many other things which Jesus did, the which, if they should be written every one, I <u>suppose</u> that even the world itself could not contain the books that should be written. Amen.

- suppose – imagine – ο ἴομαι – *Present – This is an ongoing activity in the present time of the speaker.*

"Many interpreters think that these two verses were written by some other hand than John's. Some ascribe John to two different writers. The entire chapter, though bear in unmistakable marks of John's authorship in its style and language, was probably imposed subsequently to the completion of the Gospel."

Vincent Word Studies https://biblehub.com/commentaries/vws/john/21.htm.

The Historical Background.

Inter– Testament Period – Malachi to John the Baptist is about 400 years.
New Testament Period

1. John the Baptist goes through to the lifetime of the Apostle John.
2. The Roman control of Palestine.

Cyrus the Great – 559 – 529 BC. His empire extended from the Indus River Valley in present-day Pakistan to the Mediterranean Sea before Alexander conquered it in 333– 331 BC. Cyrus permitted the rebuilding of Jerusalem. He established the local Rule by Satraps as Governors."Beyond the River" Syria., Cyrus the Great, and by Cyrus II in 546 BC. He built a great empire under the rule of Darius I and his son Xerxes.

Antiochus Epiphanes – reigned from 175 – 163 BC. He cruelly oppressed the Jews and caused them to revolt. Alexander the Great traveled from Greece. After conquering Persia, he moved south along the coast through present-day Syria, Lebanon, Israel, and Palestine. "In the summer of 332 BC, Palestine is conquered by Alexander the Great. The land and people of Israel were now part of the Hellenistic world. Alexander passed through Palestine to Gaza during his campaign to subjugate the Phoenician coast and then on his way from Egypt to Babylonia. He may have spent some time in Palestine dealing with a revolt in Samaria, and it is possible that he met then with Jewish leaders." nnnnnn

www.myjewishlearning.com/article/palestine-in-the-hellenistic-age

Alexander introduced the Greek language and culture to each nation. He invited the Jew to live in Alexandria, Egypt, and a High Priest oversaw the local government.

Maccabean Independence 64 – 40 BC. Jews won their independence and rededicated the Temple in 165 BC. The origin of the Feast of Dedication – CHANUKAH – occurs on the 25th of Kislev – Nov.– Dec.

Hasmonean Dynasty 164 – 64 BC. The Dynasty was re-established but, after some years, became corrupt and assumed the office of King as well. More significant corruption and unrest followed; disagreement about the succession in 63 BC. Rome obtained a foothold in Palestine by acting as an arbitrator through Pompey, a Roman general.

Roman Rule of Israel/Judah – 40 BC. – 70 AD.

Judea under direct Roman Rule – 63 BC – 66 AD.

Antipater – The Idumean obtained favor from Mark Anthony and succeeded in having his son.

Herod, made king of all Palestine under Roman power. Matt. 2:1– 23. His kingdom divided among three of his sons.

Antipater had four sons and one daughter, referred to as the **Herodian dynasty over Judea and Samaria.**

Herod the Great – 37– 4 BC, ruled in Jerusalem. He has gained lasting infamy as the slaughterer of the "innocents," as recounted in the New Testament book of Matthew.

Archelaus, the son of Herod the Great, 4 BC– 6 AD. And he was banished by Augustus in 6 AD.

Caesar Augustus is the Roman emperor at the time of Jesus' birth in 5/6 BC. Luke 2:1

Tiberius – Luke tells us that John the Baptist began preaching during the fifteenth year of the reign of Tiberius Caesar. 26/27 AD. See Luke 3:1– 2.

Claudius – 41 – 54 AD – poisoned. – Acts 1:27– 30.

Roman Appointees Called Procurators

1. 10 – 13 AD – M. Ambivius
2. 13 – 15 AD – Annius Rufus
3. 15 – 26 AD – Valerius Gratus – prefect of Judea & Samaria.
4. 26 – 36 AD – Pontius Pilate Luke 3:1; 23:1.
5. 36 – 36 AD – Marcellus
6. 37 – 41 AD – Herennius Capito-Galilee and Perea, on the east bank of Jordon in 4 BC -39 AD.

Herod Antipas – Luke 3:1, a tetrarch – one of the four <u>governors</u> of Iturea. North of Galilee. Mount Hermon – extreme northeast of Israel. Philip, the son of Cleopatra of Jerusalem and from Egypt. 4 BC – 34 AD. Mark 6:17.

Herod Agrippa I., the grandson of Herod the Great—37– 44 AD. [Acts 12.] ruling over nation of Israel.

"King of Judea; born about the year 10 BC. Josephus "Ant." xiv. Nine, § 2. He died suddenly in 44 AD.

"His career, with its abundant and extreme vicissitudes, illustrates remarkably the complete dependence of the royal family of Judea, even for the means of subsistence, upon the favor of the Roman emperors of the first century.*"*

www.Jewishencyclopedia.com/articles/912– agrippa– i

JUDAISM, JEWS, AND ISRAELITES.

"Keep in mind that no nation in history ever experienced such a transformation as did Judah in the Babylonian captivity. A fragment of the nation that returned to the Land forsook idolatry and indifference, and their zeal for Jehovah and His honor gave rise to what historians have called JUDAISM. Remember that a person then is called a JEW is referencing the tribe of Judah and the culture of the person, not his faith system. An Israelite refers to his spiritual connection to Abraham and Jacob."

americainclass.org/sources/becomingmodern/prosperity/text1/colcommentary.pdf

THE HIGH PRIESTS.

Since no king ruled, the High Priest was chosen as Jehovah's representative. The tradition of the Hasmoneans appointed the High Priest. Although at first, there was a civil governor, usually a Jew, but not always. The foreign overlords of Judea escalated the political power of the High Priest until that sacred office was bought and sold by not a few times the ambitious and unscrupulous.

THE SCRIBES.

A class of professional students acted as expounders of the Law known as Sopherimor – SCRIBES. They developed from the days of Ezra. They were usually pious and studious men anxious less for the spirit than for the letter of the Law.

Their interpretations became the Traditions of the Oral Law. Halakkah

Their understanding of the Oral Law.

Haggadahe – Developed by the scribes as a hedge to ensure exact obedience.

Mishna – Halakkah and the Haggadah completed about 200 AD.

Talmuds – Jerusalem and Babylonian.

THE RABBINICAL SCHOOLS.
Rabbi Hillel, c.30 BC – 10 AD.

His approach was a moderate approach to the Law. The Jerusalem Talmud calls him the president of the Sanhedrin. His approach to the Law followed until the 400s AD.

Rabbi Shammai, 50 BC to 30 AD.

His approach became a conservative approach to the Law. The school of Hillel gained ascendancy after 70 AD.

SYNAGOGUE

The Scribes developed the meeting places to legalize the nation effectively. Some method of accessible instruction was necessary. Hence, the SYNAGOGUE or a meetinghouse developed the Law, and the Prophets read and exhortations given. The Synagogue services held on Saturday, Monday, and Thursday comprised of worship, prayer, and instruction without a sacrifice.

SADDUCEES and PHARISEES

There was a great rivalry between the priests and the scribes. The priests, many of whom were corrupt and unworthy of office, claimed authority because of their official position; the scribes, often bitter, narrow, and fanatic, They claimed authority as expounders of the Law. In the days of the Maccabees and the following days, this rivalry often burst into bloodshed.

THE SADDUCEES

The Sadducees were made up mainly of the priestly class. They controlled all the religious activities on the Temple grounds. They were the aristocracy of the nation. Their power was not in their influence on the ordinary people but rather with the wealthy and politically– minded. They were the "moderns" of their day considered worldly. They had little place for God in their thoughts and plans denying the supernatural, especially the resurrection. As men of the world, their interests confined to this life only.

PHARISEES – called separatists.

They were established in about 200 BC and the time of Jesus. Comprised of 6,000 members. They were scornful, intolerant, and rallied around the scribes and commanded the respect of the common people for in observance of the Law and the Oral Law.

https://www.learnreligions.com/who-were-the-pharisees-700706

They identified with those who believed in the Torah, miracles, and the resurrection from the dead. Nicodemus is typical of this group.

PUBLICANS

They farmed the taxes (e.g., Zacchaeus, Luke 19:2) levied on from a towns or districts, and thus undertook to pay to the supreme government a certain amount of money. In order to collect the taxes, the publicans employed subordinates (5:27 ; 15:1;18:10), who, for their own ends, were often guilty of extortion and peculation. The taxes are paid to the Romans and hence regarded by the Jews as a very heavy burden, and hence also the collectors of taxes, who were Jews, were hated and were usually spoken of in very opprobrious terms. Jesus was accused of being a "friend of publicans and sinners." (*Luke 7:34.*

Edited Easton's Bible Dictionary—Publican

THE SANHEDRIN.

They were the supreme judicial council that seems to have been a gradual development after the ministry of the prophets had ceased. Josephus first mentions it in 69 BC, but it probably existed much earlier.

https://www.Jewishvirtuallibrary.org/the-sanhedrin

This body was composed of seventy men, according to the number of nations in Genesis 10. from many priests and elders who served under the High Priest. These are from the highest authority among the Jews in religious affairs and often in temporal matters. They could pass sentences but could not execute a death sentence without any Roman sanction.

https://hermeneutics.stackexchange.com/questions

A Jewish priest named Manasseh, who had married a Samaritan, chose to desert rather than obey the Governor. He helped to build the Temple on Mt. Gerazim, where they worshipped Jehova.

https://fgcp.org/content/mount-gerizim-temple-worship-part-2

He or one of his successors introduced a copy of the Law, and sacrifices are instituted.

The Jews never ceased to hold them in utmost contempt for counterfeiting the true religion of Jehovah and claiming to be descendants of the "Lost Ten Tribes." Manasseh, as presented in both the Book of Kings, commanded that the King write a copy of the Law for his use see Deut. 17:18

Bibliography and References – Websites – Misc.

Adams, John, B.D. *The Mosaic Tabernacle microform.; studies in the priesthood and the sanctuary of the Jews.* ReInk Books. 2018.

Bello, Moreno Dal. *Jesus Christ Is God.* Self– publics.lulu.com., August 31, 2018.

Bernard, John Henry. *A Critical and Exegetical Commentary on the Gospel According to St John.Vol.1.*

Bereshit Rabbah 18:1; cf. Taanit 23b *https://www.sefaria.org/Bereishit_Rabbah?lang*=bi 5 1688.

Bible History https://www.bible-story.com/Tabernacle/tab4the_entrance Gate.htm.

Chicago Manual of Style/Turabian citation. 17th ed. Turabian 9th ed.

Chkoreff, Larry. *The Flowing River.* Createspace, United States. 2011.

DeHaan, M. R. *The Tabernacle, The House of Blood.* Grand Rapids, Zondervan Publishing House. 1955.

Dilworth, John Dilworth. *The Pictorial Model of the Tabernacle; its rites and ceremonies. ReInk* Books, 2018.

Dods, Marcus. *The Gospel of St. John. The Expositor's Bible.* Hodder & Soughton, 1899.

Eckhard, John. *Rebuilding the Tabernacle of David.* Crusaders Ministries. 2004.

Edersheim, Alfred. *The Temple – Its Ministry and Services.* Kindle Publisher, Sept. 1, 1994.

Edwards, William D. *"On The Physical Death of Jesus Christ."* JAMA, March 21,1986. v 255,1.

Englishman's Greek Concordance of New Testament. Third Edition, 1860.

Eckhardt, John Author. *Rebuilding the Tabernacle of David Back to the Future.* Crusaders Ministries.

Exell, Joseph S. and Henry Donald Maurice Spence– Jones., editors. *Pulpit Commentary.* Peabody, MA. Hendrickson Publishers,1950. e– sword.

Gaebelein, Frank E, Editor, D. A. Carson Author, Walter W. Wessel Author, Walter L. Liefeld Authors, *Expositor's Bible.* Zondervan Academic, 2004. e– sword.

Fuller, Charles E. *The Tabernacle in the Wilderness.* Westwood, N. J. Fleming H. Revell, 1955.

Geneva Bible 1599-PD https://www.reformedreader.org/gbn.htm.

Gill, John. *Gill's Commentary, An Exposition of the Old and New Testaments.* 1772.

Gingrich & Arndt. *A Greek English Lexicon of the New Testament.*

Guzik, David, *Commentary on the whole Bible.* Enduring Word Media, 2012.

Harrison Norman B. *The Gospel of John.* Minneapolis, nd.

Haldeman, I.M., *The Tabernacal – Priesthood, and Offering.* Tappan, Fleming H. Revel, 1935.

Hendriksen, William. *The New Testament Commentary – Exposition of Gospel of John.* Grand Rapids, Baker Book House, 1972.

Herczeg, Rabbi Yisrael. *The Torah with Rashi Commentary.* Jewish Publication Society.

Heslup, John. *Remarks upon the Tabernacle of Moses.* ReInk Books, 2017.

Huntzinger, John. *Sinai in the Sanctuary – Mountain Theology.* Southlake, Texas. GateWay, Academic, 2017.

Ironside, H. A. *The Continual Burnt Offering.* Chicago, Loizaux, Brothers, Truth Depot, 1943.

Jamieson, Robertson, Andrew, Fausset, and David Brown. *Commentary Critical and Explanatory – Book of John (Annotated) (Commentary Critical and Explanatory on the Whole Bible 43)* Kindle edition.

Justin Martyr. *Dialogue with Trypho, the Jew, p. 69.*

King James Version 1871. e– sword.

Lange, John Peter, *Lange's Commentary on the Holy Scripture.* Wif and Stock Publishers, Revised edition. May 1, 2007.

Leslie M., John. *The Tabernacle: God Dwelt Among Men.* Kindle – Publisher, 2013.

Levine, Amy– Jill and Marc Zvi Brettler, editors. *The Jewish New Testament Commentary,* Oxford; Oxford University Press, 2011.

Levy, David M., *The Tabernacle – Shadows of the Messiah.* Bellmawr, N. J. The Friends of Israel. Gospel Ministry, 1993.

Josephus, Flavius. *Antiquities of the Jews. 18.5.2.*

Keil, Karl Friedrich and Franz Delitzsch, *Commentary on the Old Testament.*

Lightfoot, Robertson. *Robertson's, Hor, Hebr. iii. 287.*

Marcus, John F. *From Tabernacle to Church: A Deeper Study of the Tabernacle.* Essence Publishing, 1996.

Master, John R. *Timely Truths from the Tabernacle.* Regular Baptist Press, 1992.

McIlvaine, Richard K. *Enter My Rest: The Feast of Tabernacles Being Fulfilled Today.* Createspace, USA.

Meyer, F, B. *The Gospel of John.* Grand Rapids, Zondervan Publishing House, 1952.

Morgan, G. Campbell. *Morgan's Exposition on the Whole Bible – Exodus.* Revell Publishers, 1959. *https://www.studylight.org/commentaries/kdo/exodus.htm.l*

Morris, Leon. *The Gospel According to John Revised.Grand* Rapids, William B. Eerdmans Publishing Company, 1973.

Mishnah Sabbath c. 10. sect. 3.
                    https://www.meaningfullife.com/chapter-one-text-ethics-of-our-fathers/ Talmud

Nicoll, William. *The Expositor's Greek Testament 5 vols.* Hendrickson Publishers Inc, January 1, 2002.

The International Standard Bible Encyclopedia, Grand Rapids, Michigan, Wm. B. Eerdmans, Publishing Co. 1939 . *https://www.internationalstandardbible.com*

Pettingill, William L. *Into The Holiest.* Findlay, Fundamental Truth Pub.1939.

Right, Tom. *John for Everyone, Part two.* London, SPCK, 2003.

Ritchie, John. *Tabernacle in the Wilderness: A Study of Christ in the Tabernacle, the Offerings, and the Priesthood.* Christian Literature; First Edition (January 1, 1923).

Robertson's, A. T. *Robertson's Word Pictures in the New Testament.* Vols. 6. 1932. e– sword.

Ryle, J. C. *Expository Thoughts on the Gospels.* Vol. 3. p. 269. Kindle Edition. *Exposition on the Gospel of John with Notes. (ukgo.com).*

Simpson, A. B. *Christ in the Tabernacle and Leviticus.* Harrisburg, PA, Christian Publication, Inc. n.d.

Slemming, C.W. *Made According to Pattern.* Christian Literature Crusade, 1956.

Sproul, R. C., *John.* Reformation Trust Publishing, 2019.

Strong, James. *The Tabernacle of Israel: Its Structure and Symbolism.* Grand Rapids: Kregel Publications, 1987.
                    www.barnesandnoble.com/w/the– Tabernacle– of– israel– james– strong

  "One of the nineteenth century's most respected Bible scholars spent some thirty years of systematic study in preparing The Tabernacle of Israel.

Talmud – *Mishna Avot 1 and Sotah 20a *Safaria – Nederim 31a*
                    https://www.meaningfullife.com/chapter-one-text-ethics-of-our-fathers/ Talmud

Thompson, Llewllyn. *God's Method of Worship*. Reynoldsburg, Ohio, nd.

Thayer, Joseph. *Thayer's Greek – English Lexicon of the New Testament*. Hendrickson Publishers. 1996.

Vincent, Marvin R. *The Word Studies in the New Testament*. 4 Vols, 1887. *https://biblehub.com/commentaries/john/1-20.htm.*

Vine, W. F. *Expository Dictionary of Old and New Testament Words*. Fleming H. Revell Company. 1981.

Wallace, Daniel. Greek Grammar – *Beyond the Basics*. Grand Rapids, MI, Zondervan,1996.

Yee, Gale A. *Jewish Feasts and the Gospel of John*. Oregon. Wipf & Stock, 1989.

Zehr, Paul M. *Glimpses of the Tabernacle*. Mennonite Information Center, Lancaster, PA, 1976.

Web Sites concerning the Tabernacle found on the internet.

ww.bible – history.com
https://biblestudentsdaily.com
http://learn.conservativeyeshiva.org/yoma– chapter– five– mishnah– one/, http://www. newadvent.org/fathers/01286.htm.
https://www.sefaria.org/Mishnah_Shabbat.3?lang=bi
https://www.meaningfullife.com/chapter-one-text-ethics-of-our-fathers/ Talmud https://www. google.com/ &q=Safaria%E2%80%93Nederim++31a++MISH http://learn.conservativeyeshiva. org/shabbat– /Misnah Sabbath c.10 sect. 3.
https://www.studylight.org/commentaries/kdo/exodus.htm.l.
https://www.studylight.org/commentaries/kdo/exodus.htm.l
https://www.sefaria.org/Mishnah_Shabbat.3?lang=bi https://www.meaningfullife.com/chapter-one-text-ethics-of-our-fathers/ Talmud
http://learn.conservativeyeshiva.org

Misc. works concerning the Tabernacle found on the internet.

Adams, John. *The Mosaic Tabernacle; studies in the priesthood and the sanctuary of the Jews*. Published by ReInk Books,1900.

Chkoreff, Larry. *The Flowing River.* Createspace, United States. 2011.

Dilworth, John. *The Pictorial Model of the Tabernacle; its rites and ceremonies.* S N Books World, ReInk Books, 2018.

Eckhardt, John. *Rebuilding the Tabernacle of David Back to the Future.* Crusaders Ministries, 2004.

Gombarashama, MR Justice. *Inside Deep Waters of Salvation: Amazing God s Grace.*

> Createspace Independent Publishing Platform, 2014.
> "This is when the earthly Tabernacle is restored to its original form as it was formed ithe beginning, immortality, incorruptibility, and holiness will be restored. When man's body becomes the true habitation of God s Spirit, divinity is experienced."

Hendriksen, William *"Passover or Pentecost or Tabernacles." www.christianbook.com*

Heslup, John. *Remarks upon the Tabernacle of Moses.* ReInk Books. 2017.

Leslie, John, M. *The Tabernacle: God Dwelt Among Men.* 2013.

Marcus, John F. *From Tabernacle to Church: A Deeper Study of the Tabernacle.* Essence Publishing. Jan. 1, 1996.

Master, John R. Timely Truths from the Tabernacle. Regular Baptist Press, Reno, NV. 1992. McIlvaine, Richard K. *Enter My Rest: The Feast of Tabernacles Being Fulfilled Today.* Book Depository International. London, United Kingdom. 2011.

Ritchie, John. *Tabernacle in the Wilderness: A Study of Christ in the Tabernacle, the Offerings, and the Priesthood.* Publisher of Christian Literature; 7th edition. Jan. 1, 1923.

Tozer, A. W. *Renewed Day by Day.* Pub. unknown.

Selected Introductory Quotes

Henry, Mathew. *Commentary on Exodus* "2. God himself would furnish him with the model: According to all that I show thee, vs. 9. God showed him an exact plan of it, in miniature, which he must conform to in all points."

"There is in the midst of these instructions an express caution given to Moses, to take heed of varying from his model: Make them after the pattern shown thee, v. 40. Nothing was left to his own invention, or the fancy of the workmen, or the people's humour; but the will of God must be religiously observed in every particular. Thus, 1. All God's providences are exactly according to his counsels, and the copy never varies from the original. Infinite Wisdom never changes its measures; whatever is purposed shall undoubtedly be performed."

https://st– akla.org/bible/commentary/en/ot/matthewhenry/exodus/ch25.htm.l

Jamieson, Robert. The Second Book of Moses, Called Exodus. Independently Published. nd. 25:1– 40. CONCERNING AN OFFERING 8. a sanctuary that I may dwell among them. In one sense the Tabernacle was to be a palace, the royal residence of the King of Israel, in which He was to dwell among His people, receive their petitions, and issue His responses. But it was also to be a place of worship, in which God was to record His name and to enshrine the mystic symbols of His presence. *https://ccel.org/ccel/jamieson/jfb/jfb.x.ii. xxv.htm.*

Pink, Arthur. *Gleanings In Exodus – 33. The Tabernacle*

"The Tabernacle was a symbol of God's dwelling. There is a Sanctuary, wherein is the especial residence and manifestation of the glorious presence of God."
"Tabernacle is a type of the Lord Jesus Himself, particularly of Him here on earth during the days of His flesh."

https://bible.prayer request.com/7789– works– of– arthur– pink– 400– books

Spurgeon, C. H. A Sermon No. 267. Sabbath Morning, August 14th, 1859 "UNDER THE OLD Mosaic dispensation God had a visible dwelling placeamong men. The bright shekinah was seen between the wings of the cherubim which overshadowed the mercy– seat; and in the Tabernacle . . ."

https://www.blueletterbible.org/Comm/spurgeon_charles/sermons/0267.cfm.

The Mediator—The Interpreter – A Sermon No. 2097. Lord's– day Morning, July 28th, 1888. ". . . the Lord has ways of communing with His people which fill them with fear; but secondly, this endears the Mediator to them; and thirdly, this Mediator teaches them to interpret wisely the Lord's darker dealings with them . . ."

https://archive.spurgeon.org/sermons/2097.php.

Printed in the United States
by Baker & Taylor Publisher Services